HOUGHTON MIFFLIN HARCOURT

JOURNEYS

Write-In Reader
Grade 3

Printed in the U.S.A.

ISBN: 978-0-547-25417-3

3456789- 0877- 17 16 15 14 13 12 11 10

4500227772 B C D E F

HOUGHTON MIFFLIN HARCOURT
School Publishers

Contents

✓ **TARGET VOCABULARY**

certainly
fine
proud
strolled

Athens, Greece

Check the answer.

1 Long ago, Athens, Greece, had many beautiful buildings. The people of Athens were _____ of their city.

☐ **sore** ☐ **proud** ☐ **empty**

2 People often met outdoors. They _____ through the streets. They stood in the marketplace. They talked about ideas and art.

☐ **strolled** ☐ **overlooked** ☐ **accepted**

3 Even today, Athens is _____ a place worth visiting. Visitors are sure to enjoy the statues and buildings from long ago.

☐ **lonely** ☐ **special** ☐ **certainly**

2

Ancient Greek Empire
Macedonia   Thrace   Black Sea

Persian empire

Athens
Sparta   Mediterranean sea

4 **Describe how a <u>fine</u> day would look to you.**

_____

_____

_____

5 **Tell about a place where you <u>strolled</u> recently.**

_____

_____

_____

Icos Goes to School

by Margaret Maugenest

Morning, 400 B.C.E.
Athens, Greece

Doran shook the sleeping boy. "Time to get up, Icos," he said. "It's going to be **fine**, sunny weather."

Icos yawned and turned over. "It's always fine weather in Athens," he said. "So what?"

"You must get up," Doran said firmly. "It's time for school."

Stop | Think | Write

STORY STRUCTURE

When and where does the story take place?

_____

_____

_____

4

Icos sighed. It was barely light out. He didn't want to get up. It took him a while to get out of bed.

Doran walked to school with Icos. Doran was Icos's servant. The two **strolled** through the streets.

They reached the school late. The teacher was already sitting on his tall chair. Icos sat on a bench at the back. Doran stayed outside.

Stop **Think** **Write**

CAUSE AND EFFECT

Why doesn't Icos rush to get ready?

_____

_____

_____

The teacher gave each student a block of wax. It was time to practice writing. Icos looked for his stylus.

Doran came in with the stylus. Now Icos could carve letters into the wax. Icos tried not to yawn. He was **proud** of his tidy writing. He wanted to do a good job.

Stop | Think | Write

VOCABULARY

What are you <u>proud</u> of that you can do well?

_____

_____

_____

By now, Icos was wide awake. It was time to learn a poem. This poem was not written down. The teacher spoke each line. The students repeated it.

The teacher called on Icos to say the whole poem. Icos stood. He spoke in a firm voice. He did not leave one word out.

Doran came in. He took the writing stylus back. "You **certainly** did well!" he told Icos.

Stop Think Write

VOCABULARY

What other word could Doran use that has the same meaning as certainly?

_____

_____

_____

Now it was music time. One student played the harp. Another played the flute. Icos and the other boys sang.

Icos looked out at the servants. Doran was nodding in time to the music. The teacher was tapping his foot. "We must be doing well," Icos thought.

CAUSE AND EFFECT

Stop **Think** **Write**

What makes Icos think that the students are playing the music well?

_____

_____

_____

8

The afternoon was for sports. The boys walked to the sports field. Their servants came with them. The field was at the edge of the city.

The boys worked hard. Building strong bodies was important. They ran races. They jumped. Sports teachers watched them. Icos won a race. He was very pleased.

Stop **Think** **Write**

STORY STRUCTURE

Where do the boys practice sports?

_____

_____

_____

At last the school day ended. Icos and Doran walked home together. "That was a full day," Icos said.

"Yes, it was," Doran agreed. "You had fun at school, didn't you?" he asked.

Icos knew what Doran was saying. "Yes, I did. I'll try not to be so slow and grumpy tomorrow morning!"

Stop | Think | Write

How does Icos feel about his day?

_____

_____

_____

_____

Look Back and Respond

1 Name one way that Doran is helpful to Icos.

Hint
For clues, see pages 4, 6, and 7.

_____

_____

_____

2 How does Icos change at the end of the story?

Hint
For clues, see page 10.

_____

_____

_____

3 What clues in the pictures show that the story takes place long ago?

Hint
Clues are on every page.

_____

_____

_____

Lesson 2

✓ **TARGET VOCABULARY**

guilty
honest
jury
trial

What Happens in a Court?

1 What if a person is accused of a crime? She might say, "I am not **guilty**." In a court, people try to find out if she is telling the truth.

What other word could someone use to say that she is not _guilty_?

_____

2 A **trial** gives both sides a chance to tell what they believe happened. Lawyers ask questions to try to learn the truth.

Why is it important to hear both sides in a _trial_?

_____

_____

_____

3 Most people try very hard to be **honest** in court. They tell the truth when a question is asked.

Write a word that means the opposite of <u>honest</u>.

_____

4 Twelve people are on the **jury**. They decide if the person did the crime or not. Everyone on the jury must agree.

Why do you think a <u>jury</u> has twelve people?

_____

_____

_____

The Trial of John Peter Zenger

by Lois Grippo

A Stamp for Eastchester

School children in the town of Eastchester, New York, want a special postage stamp. They want a stamp of a man named John Peter Zenger. John Zenger was once put on **trial** in Eastchester. He was put on trial because he told the truth!

Stop	Think	Write

CONCLUSIONS

Why was the trial of John Peter Zenger unusual?

_____

_____

_____

An Unfair Leader

The trial of John Peter Zenger took place in 1735. America was still part of England. The governor of New York was a man named William Cosby. People in New York did not pick Cosby. He was sent from England.

William Cosby would not let some men vote. This made people in Eastchester very angry. They wanted others to know that Cosby was unfair.

Stop Think Write

INFER AND PREDICT

Why might people want a governor they choose themselves?

_____

_____

_____

15

John Peter Zenger Speaks Out

John Peter Zenger ran a newspaper. He wrote in his paper about William Cosby. Everyone who read the paper learned of Governor Cosby's unfair actions.

Governor Cosby had Zenger put in jail! He said that the stories in Zenger's newspaper told lies. He claimed that the lies hurt him. Zenger stayed in jail for ten months before he even had a trial.

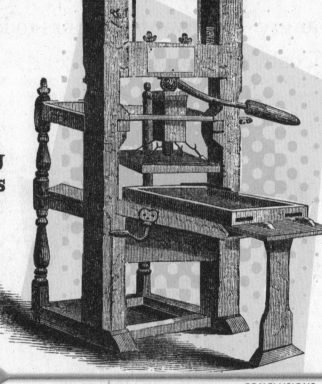

a printing press

| Stop | Think | Write |

CONCLUSIONS

Do you think that William Cosby was a good governor? Explain.

_____

_____

_____

16

Trial by Jury

At last the trial began. A **jury** would decide if John Zenger was guilty. Did he tell lies that hurt Governor Cosby? If he did, the jury would have to say he was guilty.

The jury heard the governor's side of the story first. They heard about Zenger's newspaper stories. They were told that no one had the right to print bad things about the governor.

Stop | **Think** | **Write**

VOCABULARY

What was the job of the **jury** in John Peter Zenger's trial?

_____

_____

_____

Zenger's Story

A lawyer told John Zenger's side of the story. "What you heard was true," he said. "The stories in the paper did say bad things about the governor."

The lawyer didn't stop there. "However, the stories were **honest**," he said. "They told the truth about what Governor Cosby did."

Stop | Think | Write

VOCABULARY

Why do newspaper reporters have to be <u>honest</u> when they report the news?

_____

_____

_____

A Big Decision

Finally, both sides were finished. The people on the jury thought about all they had heard. Then they made their decision.

It only took the jury ten minutes to make up their minds. They said that John Peter Zenger was not **guilty**!

Stop **Think** **Write**

INFER AND PREDICT

Why do you think that the jury found John Peter Zenger not guilty?

_____

_____

_____

Remembering a Leader

John Peter Zenger was a leader. The men in the jury were leaders, too. They stood up for the right to tell the truth.

That is why the children of Eastchester want a postage stamp. They want to remind us of the trial of John Peter Zenger. They want to remind us of a right that keeps our country strong.

Stop | **Think** | **Write**

CONCLUSIONS

Do you think that a stamp of John Peter Zenger is a good idea? Explain.

_____

_____

_____

Look Back and Respond

1 How was John Peter Zenger a leader? Explain.

Hint

For clues, see pages 16 and 20.

_____

_____

_____

2 Why do you think the jury took only ten minutes to decide that John Peter Zenger was not guilty?

Hint

For clues, see page 18.

_____

_____

_____

3 How do the children of Eastchester show that they care about people from their town's past?

Hint

For clues, see page 14.

_____

_____

_____

contacted
customers
earn
figure

Neighbors Working Together

1 A neighborhood can be a street. It can be more than one street. Good neighbors **figure** out ways to help one another.

Tell about a time when you had to figure out a way to do something.

_____

_____

_____

2 Some people wanted to make their neighborhood look better. They **contacted** their neighbors. They met to talk about what they could do.

How have you contacted your friends?

_____

_____

_____

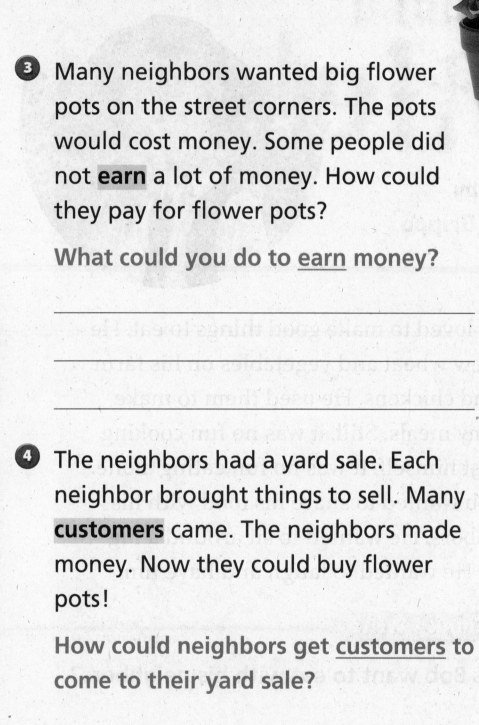

3 Many neighbors wanted big flower pots on the street corners. The pots would cost money. Some people did not **earn** a lot of money. How could they pay for flower pots?

What could you do to earn money?

_____

_____

_____

4 The neighbors had a yard sale. Each neighbor brought things to sell. Many **customers** came. The neighbors made money. Now they could buy flower pots!

How could neighbors get customers to come to their yard sale?

_____

_____

_____

Not Just a Little!

by
Lois Grippo

Bob loved to make good things to eat. He grew wheat and vegetables on his farm. He had chickens. He used them to make yummy meals. Still, it was no fun cooking for just himself. It was no fun eating alone.

Bob wanted to share his food with his neighbors. He wanted to sit around a big table. He wanted to laugh and have fun.

Stop **Think** **Write**

UNDERSTANDING CHARACTERS

Why does Bob want to eat with his neighbors?

_____

_____

_____

Bob called his neighbor Luis. "Can you come to my house for dinner?" Bob asked.

"I cannot leave the store," Luis said. "I am staying open late to **earn** more money."

Luis sold fruit and vegetables. He never made time to talk or have fun. Bob called his other neighbors. They were busy, too. Bob sat on his porch and thought. He tried to **figure** out a way to get his neighbors together.

Stop **Think** **Write**

VOCABULARY

How does Luis <u>earn</u> money?

_____

_____

_____

Bob came up with a plan. He cooked chicken in a pot. It smelled very good. Bob went to the park with his pot of chicken.

Bob walked past Luis's store. The door was open. Luis smelled the chicken. He came outside and saw Bob.

"What is making that good smell?" Luis asked.

"The smell is the chicken in my pot," said Bob.

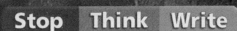

Stop **Think** **Write**

INFER AND PREDICT

Why do you think Bob doesn't eat his chicken at home?

_____

_____

_____

"There is a picnic at four o'clock," Bob said. "You must come! You can bring some food. Tell your **customers** to come, too."

"I am too busy for a picnic. I have to work," said Luis. Then he smelled the chicken again. "Maybe I will close the store early. I can bring a little corn to the picnic."

"No, no! Not just a little!" said Bob. "Bring lots of corn!"

Stop Think Write

VOCABULARY

Name three things <u>customers</u> might buy in Luis's store.

_____

_____

_____

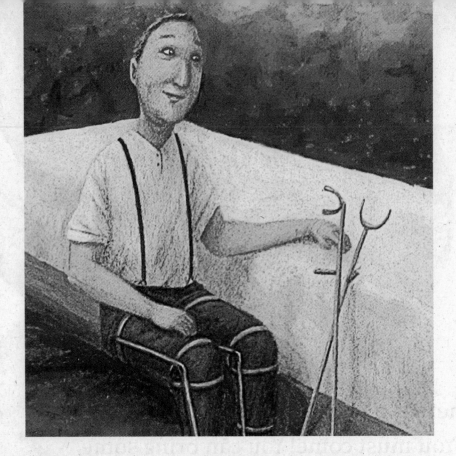

Bob went on his way. He stopped at the library. He stopped at the hardware store. Everyone smelled Bob's chicken. They all wanted to come to the picnic.

At last, Bob arrived at the park. He put his chicken on the table. Bob's neighbor Lee came by.

Stop | Think | Write

INFER AND PREDICT

Why does Bob stop at the library and the hardware store?

_____

_____

_____

28

"Luis **contacted** me. He told me there is a picnic. I will bring a little bit of milk," Lee said.

"No, no! Not just a little!" said Bob. "Bring lots of milk."

At four o'clock, Lee came back to the park. He brought lots of milk. Luis came to the park with lots of corn.

Stop | **Think** | **Write**

VOCABULARY

How might Luis have <u>contacted</u> Lee?

_____

_____

_____

More and more people came to the park. They all brought lots of food. Soon the picnic became a grand party.

Everyone had fun. Everyone talked and laughed together. Bob was happy. His plan worked just fine.

Stop **Think** **Write**

What was Bob's plan?

_____

_____

_____

Look Back and Respond

1 Write three things to tell about Bob.

Hint

Look for clues on page 24.

_____

_____

_____

2 Write two things to tell about Luis.

Hint

Look for clues on page 25.

_____

_____

_____

3 How are Bob and Luis alike?

Hint

Look on pages 26 and 27. Do you think Luis likes eating tasty food?

_____

_____

_____

People Working Together

A new park is about to open. It needs a nature trail. A **crew** of helpers clears the land for a path.

A creek goes across the trail. The helpers will build a bridge. It will **stretch** across the creek.

The ranger puts a log over the creek. He walks across it. He is good at **balancing** on things. He does not fall.

The helpers add more logs. They use rope to hold the logs together. Soon the bridge is done. The workers are filled with **excitement**.

1 A _____ of people can make a bridge. They work together to build it.

2 The workers are all full of

_____ when they

finish the bridge.

3 A person who is not good at

_____ might fall.

4 How can you tell when someone is full of <u>excitement</u>?

_____

_____

_____

5 Why does a bridge have to <u>stretch</u> from one side of the creek to the other?

_____

_____

Building a New Barn

by Margaret Maugenest

The farmer looks at her barn. Once, the barn looked good. The wood boards were straight. The roof was strong.

Now the barn is old. The planks sag. The roof is sinking in. The paint is chipped.

The farmer is not happy. She wants to build a new barn.

Stop | Think | Write

COMPARE AND CONTRAST

How did the barn look when it was new? How does the barn look now?

_____

_____

_____

Getting Started

A **crew** of helpers comes. Some of the workers are from town. Some of them come from other farms. They are all ready to work!

First, they tear down the old barn. The workers take away the used planks.

Some people chop down nearby trees. They saw the wood into planks. The new planks will be used to build the barn.

Stop **Think** **Write**

VOCABULARY

How does a <u>crew</u> help when there are many tasks to do?

_____

_____

_____

Everyone Helps!

Some people will build the barn. There are other jobs, too. The workers will get hungry. So some people will make lunch for them.

A few workers brought their children. The children watch. They will see how a barn is built. Some day they may build a barn.

| Stop | Think | Write |

MAIN IDEAS AND DETAILS

Why doesn't everyone help build the barn?

_____

_____

_____

_____

The Work Begins

To begin, workers place big blocks of stone in the ground. These will make the base of the barn.

Next, the builders make a frame for each wall. They measure the wood. Then they saw it into pieces.

The pieces are joined together. The team uses nails. The nails are metal. Sometimes they use pegs. The pegs are carved from wood.

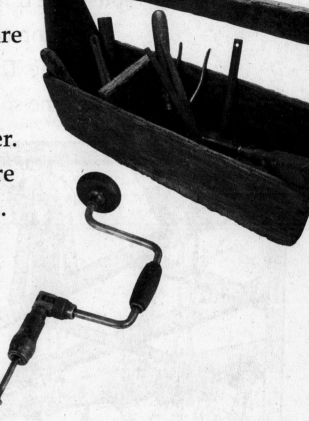

Stop | **Think** | **Write**

COMPARE AND CONTRAST

Compare nails and pegs. How are they different? How are they the same?

_____

_____

_____

Step by Step

Soon it is time to raise the barn. Workers lift the frames by hand. It is hard work. They need help. So other workers use long poles to push the frames into place.

The top comes next. Some workers climb the frame. They must be good at **balancing** on the frame so they do not fall off.

MAIN IDEAS AND DETAILS

How are the frames raised and pushed into place?

_____

_____

_____

The workers pull up long planks of wood. The planks **stretch** across the top of the barn. They fit into slots in the frame.

All the parts are nailed down. Now the roof will be very strong. Some barn roofs are slanted. Others are curved. This roof is curved.

Stop **Think** **Write**

SEQUENCE OF EVENTS

What happens after the workers fit the wood planks into the frame?

_____

_____

_____

A New Barn!

The workers stop for lunch. Then they go back to work. It is almost dark when the last nail is hammered into place. The workers feel **excitement**. They are happy and smiling. The barn is finished!

The new barn looks great. The farmer is very happy. She thanks everyone.

The workers are tired. They walk to their cars and trucks, and they go home.

Stop | **Think** | **Write**

CAUSE AND EFFECT

Why do the workers feel <u>excitement</u>?

_____

_____

_____

Look Back and Respond

1 Compare what the children do with what the grownups do.

Hint

For clues, see page 36.

_____

_____

_____

2 How does the farmer feel at the beginning of the story? How does she feel at the end? Why?

Hint

For clues, see pages 34 and 40.

_____

_____

_____

3 How do you think the workers on the team began learning how to build barns?

Hint

For clues, see page 36.

_____

_____

_____

Baseball

1 The first baseball **league** had nine teams. They began to play each other in 1871. Today, Major League Baseball has two leagues.

In what kind of sports league would you like to play?

_____

_____

_____

2 **Fans** cheer for their favorite baseball teams. Fans go crazy when their team scores a run.

Are you and your friends fans of something? Explain.

_____

_____

_____

3 The best teams in the leagues play in the World Series. In 2007, the Boston Red Sox played against the Colorado Rockies. An announcer **pronounced** the names of the players before each game.

Tell about a time someone pronounced your name wrong.

_____

_____

_____

4 People sit in the **stands** at baseball games. Fans can often buy drinks or food to eat while they watch the game.

What would you eat in the stands at a baseball game?

_____

_____

_____

Let's Play Ball!

by Lois Grippo

Baseball for Kids

Kids all over the United States love to play baseball. Most towns have a **league** for children. Teams play baseball in the spring and summer.

Boys and girls play on the teams. They play other teams from nearby towns. The players' friends and families watch from the **stands**.

Stop | **Think** | **Write**

VOCABULARY

How is a <u>league</u> different from a team?

_____

_____

_____

44

The Beginning of Little League

Baseball leagues for kids did not always exist. A man named Carl Stotz started the Little League about 70 years ago. Carl loved baseball. He thought baseball was good for kids. It was a great way to teach teamwork.

Carl's neighbors thought so, too. They raised $35 to start three teams. They got stores to donate uniforms. Carl called it the Little League.

Stop | **Think** | **Write**

CAUSE AND EFFECT

How did Carl's neighbors help start the Little League?

_____

_____

_____

Little League Then and Now

The very first Little League game was played on June 6, 1939. The Lundy Lumber team played against the Lycoming Dairy team. Lundy Lumber won.

Today, Little League teams play in every state. They play in 80 countries, too. Little League is the biggest organized sports program in the world.

Stop | **Think** | **Write**

Do you think Little League is more popular now than in 1939? Explain.

_____

_____

_____

Learning Skills

Baseball players learn many skills. They must hit the ball with the bat. They must run fast around the bases. Players need to catch balls. They have to tag runners and throw the ball to other players.

One player can't win a game alone. Kids learn to work as a team. They practice, and they get better. They learn to count on each other.

Stop | Think | Write

CAUSE AND EFFECT

When players practice as a team, what are some ways they improve?

_____

_____

_____

Going to the Big Leagues

Some great baseball players got started in Little League. One of them was Cal Ripken, Jr. He played for the Baltimore Orioles.

Baltimore **fans** loved Ripken. They cheered when the announcer **pronounced** his name. Ripken played in 2,632 straight games! He is in the Baseball Hall of Fame.

Stop | **Think** | **Write**

How did <u>fans</u> show that they loved Cal Ripken?

_____

_____

_____

Life After Little League

Many Little League players do not become great baseball players. Some go on to do other important work. Krissy Wendell became a great hockey player. Her team won a silver medal in the Olympics.

One Little League player even went on to become Vice President of the United States! Little League teaches teamwork skills. Kids can use these skills all their lives.

Stop Think Write

CONCLUSIONS

Tell about a job where it is important to work as a team. Explain.

_____

_____

_____

Who Can Belong to Little League?

- Boys and girls, ages nine to twelve, can join.

- At first, just boys could play.

- After 1974, girls could join, too.

Little Leaguers in the Baseball Hall of Fame

Nolan Ryan: Pitcher, Texas Rangers

Tom Seaver: Pitcher, New York Mets

Carl Yastrzemski: Outfielder, Boston Red Sox

Johnny Bench: Catcher, Cincinnati Reds

Roberto Clemente: Outfielder, Pittsburgh Pirates

Stop **Think** **Write**

INFER AND PREDICT

What do you think a player must do to be in the Baseball Hall of Fame?

_____

_____

_____

Look Back and Respond

1 How do you think fans affect the way teams play baseball?

_____

_____

_____

Hint

Think about how you feel when people cheer you on.

2 Why did Carl Stotz think baseball was good for kids?

_____

_____

_____

Hint

Look on page 45.

3 How can you tell that Carl's neighbors thought Little League was a good idea?

_____

_____

_____

Hint

Look on page 45.

collect
rapidly
scrambled
sorted

Collecting

Maria and Luis liked to **collect** things. Every day they walked on the beach. They picked up shells and stones.

Maria and Luis **scrambled** their shells and stones together. "Everything is mixed up," said Maria. "Let's make this neater."

She and Luis **sorted** the things into two groups. One group had shells. The other group had stones.

Maria and Luis worked **rapidly**. Soon they were done. Now everything looked neat.

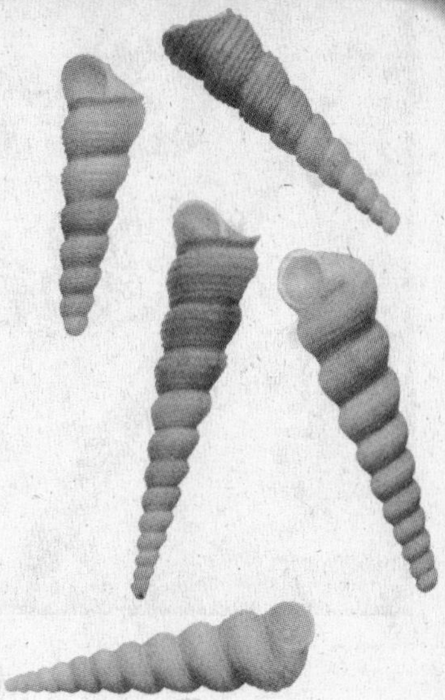

1 The kids _____
shells and stones by mixing them
together.

2 Maria and Luis worked

_____ to sort the items.

3 Maria and Luis liked to

_____ things on the

beach.

4 The kids _____ items into
two groups.

5 Name one thing you like to <u>collect</u>.

_____

6 What do you do <u>rapidly</u>?

_____

_____

_____

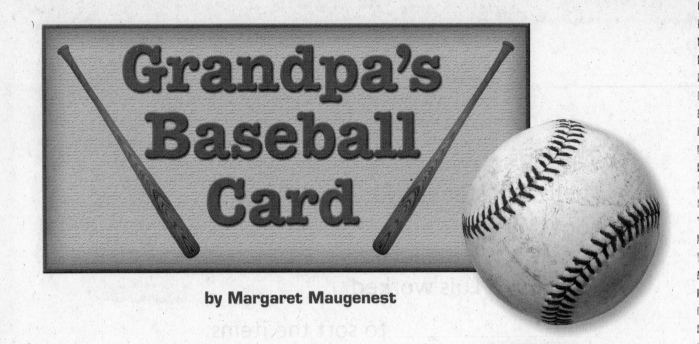

Grandpa's Baseball Card

by Margaret Maugenest

Abe had to write a report. It had to tell about someone he thought was great.

Abe loved basketball. He liked to **collect** cards of the best players. "I will write about a basketball player," he thought.

Stop | Think | Write

What does Abe like to collect?

_____

_____

_____

Abe took out his cards. They were **sorted** into groups. Each group had players from one team. Abe did not like his cards **scrambled** together.

After dinner, Abe told his mom about the report.

"I know you collect cards," she said. "Here is a new card for you."

Abe looked at the card. It was of Willie Mays. He was a great baseball player.

Stop **Think** **Write**

VOCABULARY

How are Abe's cards <u>sorted</u>?

_____

_____

_____

"My father gave me this card," said his mom. "I want you to have it."

Abe's mom began to talk about Willie Mays and baseball. Long ago, she and Abe's grandpa had watched Mays play baseball on TV.

Abe listened closely. However, baseball was not his favorite sport. "I do not know a lot about baseball," he said. "I like basketball more than any other sport!"

Stop **Think** **Write**

CONCLUSIONS

Do you think Abe likes the baseball card? Why?

_____

_____

_____

56

All week, Abe thought about the baseball card and his report. Maybe I will write about Willie Mays, he thought.

On Saturday, Abe decided to go to the library. Along the way, he stopped at the sports card store. Mr. Morgan was the owner. He was behind the counter.

"Hi, Abe," said Mr. Morgan. "Are you here for a new basketball card?"

Stop **Think** **Write**

SEQUENCE OF EVENTS

Where does Abe go before he goes to the library?

_____

_____

_____

"No," said Abe. "I want to show you something."

Abe gave the Willie Mays card to Mr. Morgan. He looked at the card a long time. Then he looked at Abe. "This is a very special card," said Mr. Morgan. "I would trade you all the cards in my store for this card."

"Wow, really?" said Abe.

"Really!" said Mr. Morgan.

Abe smiled. "No thanks," he said. "I'm going to keep it."

Stop | Think | Write

INFER AND PREDICT

How do you know the baseball card is important?

_____

_____

_____

It was getting late. Abe raced out of the store. He walked **rapidly** to the library.

Abe rushed inside. "What is the hurry?" asked Mr. Diaz. He was in charge of the library.

Abe showed the card to Mr. Diaz. "I want to write a report about Willie Mays," said Abe. "Will you help me learn about him?"

Mr. Diaz and Abe went online. They looked up Willie Mays. Mr. Diaz printed out an article.

Stop Think Write

SEQUENCE OF EVENTS

What do Mr. Diaz and Abe do after Abe asks for help?

_____

_____

_____

Mr. Diaz began to read. "Many people thought that Willie Mays was the best baseball player of the 1960s."

"What was so good about him?" asked Abe.

"He could hit the ball far," said Mr. Diaz. "Once, he hit four home runs in one game!"

Abe felt lucky to have his grandpa's baseball card. He couldn't wait to start writing the report about Willie Mays.

Stop | **Think** | **Write**

How does Abe feel after he learns more about Willie Mays?

_____

_____

_____

Look Back and Respond

1 What does Abe do before dinner?

_____

_____

_____

Hint

For a clue, see page 55.

2 Where does Abe go after the sports card store?

_____

_____

_____

Hint

For a clue, see page 59.

3 Write two things that Abe learned about Willie Mays.

_____

_____

_____

Hint

For a clue, see page 60.

illustrate
imagine
sketches
tools

Words and Pictures in Books

Check the answer.

1 An artist can _____ a story with pictures. The pictures help you understand the story.

☐ illustrate ☐ murmur ☐ cling

2 An artist can draw something from real life. An artist can _____ something to draw, too. Then the artist will draw a made-up picture.

☐ raise ☐ stretch ☐ imagine

3 Some artists make quick drawings first. These _____ may not show a lot of details.

☐ customers ☐ sketches ☐ tools

4 What are some drawing <u>tools</u> you might have at home?

_____

_____

_____

5 How would you <u>illustrate</u> a story about trees?

_____

_____

_____

Caw Caw

Douglas Florian's Books

by Gail Mack

The Boy Who Loved Drawing

Douglas Florian wasn't the first artist in his family. His dad was.

Douglas's dad loved to make **sketches** of things in nature. He showed Douglas how to draw. He taught Douglas how to look closely at nature.

Stop Think Write

INFER AND PREDICT

What things in nature can someone draw or paint?

_____

_____

_____

Drawing was fun for Douglas. When he was ten years old, he entered a coloring contest. His art won second place. His prize was a pair of roller skates.

Stop | **Think** | **Write**

CAUSE AND EFFECT

Why did Douglas win a prize?

_____

_____

_____

An Art Student

One summer, Douglas took an art class. He loved it. He learned to use different art **tools**. Artists use many tools. They might use paint or pen and ink. They might even use chalk.

Douglas was just fifteen years old. He already knew what he wanted to become. He was going to be an artist.

Stop | **Think** | **Write**

What kinds of <u>tools</u> might an artist use?

_____

_____

_____

A Working Artist

Douglas did become an artist. He sold his drawings to magazines and newspapers. He made art for children's books, too.

At first, he would **illustrate** other people's stories. Later, he wrote his own stories. His first books were about nature. Douglas filled them with drawings of things like frogs, turtles, and shells.

Stop | **Think** | **Write**

VOCABULARY

What do people do when they <u>illustrate</u> a story?

_____

_____

_____

A Writer of Poems

One day, Douglas saw a book of silly poems. He smiled as he turned the pages. "A book like this would be fun to make!" he thought.

So he wrote some poems. He used funny sounds and silly words. He made enough poems to fill a book. Then he drew pictures for the poems.

Stop | Think | Write

TEXT AND GRAPHIC FEATURES

How does the picture show a funny sound?

_____

_____

_____

Poetry Award

A Winner

Douglas liked to **imagine** made-up animals. He wrote a book of poems about them. After that, he wrote a book of poems about real animals. It was called *Beast Feast*. His books were a big hit. One book even won an award!

Douglas still loves making art and writing poems. His books make kids laugh.

Stop **Think** **Write**

TEXT AND GRAPHIC FEATURES

What detail in the text does the picture of Douglas Florian show?

_____

_____

_____

Douglas Florian Timeline

This timeline shows events in Douglas Florian's life.

1950   Douglas Florian is born.

1960   He wins second prize in an art contest.

1965   He decides to become an artist.

Around 1970   He studies art in college.

1994   His poem book, *Beast Feast*, comes out.

1995   *Beast Feast* wins the Lee Bennett Hopkins Poetry Award.

Stop | Think | Write

TEXT AND GRAPHIC FEATURES

What is one event on the timeline that you don't read about anywhere else in this story?

_____

_____

_____

Look Back and Respond

1 What did Douglas Florian do after he made pictures for other people's stories?

Hint

Look on page 67.

_____

_____

_____

2 How did Douglas Florian's dad help him become an artist?

Hint

Look on page 64.

_____

_____

_____

3 Write three words that tell about Douglas Florian's art. Explain.

Hint

Clues are on almost every page!

_____

_____

_____

advice
ashamed
harvest
serious

Planting a Garden

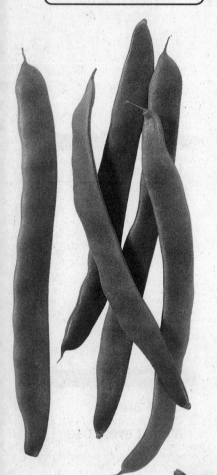

It was time to plant my garden. My friends gave lots of **advice**. They said I should plant corn, lettuce, and squash.

I planted only beans. "You are so **serious** about beans!" my friend Yolanda said. "Why only beans?"

Do you want to know the truth? I hadn't looked carefully at the seed packs. I was **ashamed** to admit my mistake. "I like beans," I said. "I like them a lot!"

I went to work. I weeded and watered. I had a good **harvest**. I ate beans for a month. Next year, I don't think I'll plant any beans.

1 People like to give _____ that they think will help you.

2 During a _____, you gather crops that have grown.

3 If you are _____ about gardening, you work hard to make your garden grow.

4 Write a word that means the opposite of <u>ashamed</u>.

_____

5 Tell about a time when someone gave you <u>advice</u>.

_____

_____

_____

73

Living Things Are Linked

A Retelling of an African Tale

by Dina McClellan

Once there was a chief who was a stern ruler. He demanded that all in the village obey him. Anyone who did not was punished terribly.

Only one person was not afraid of the chief. That was his grandmother. Who knows why the chief did not punish her. Maybe he just didn't take notice of her.

Stop | Think | Write

CONCLUSIONS

How can you tell the chief is a stern ruler?

_____

_____

_____

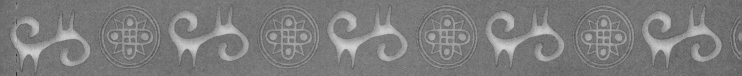

One night the chief couldn't sleep. The frogs outside were making too much noise. This was a **serious** problem for the chief.

He woke up all the people in the village. "If I can't sleep, no one will sleep," he said. "Kill all the frogs!"

Stop | **Think** | **Write**

CAUSE AND EFFECT

Why can't the chief sleep?

_____

_____

_____

So the people killed all the frogs. Later they felt **ashamed**. They did not like what they had done. They were all afraid of the chief.

Only the chief's grandmother was not afraid. "You'll be sorry," she said. "All living things are linked. Even you and the frogs."

The chief had to laugh. "How could frogs be linked to a big chief like me?" he said.

Stop | Think | Write

Why do you think people feel <u>ashamed</u> of killing the frogs?

_____

_____

_____

Soon it was time for the **harvest.**
Everyone in the village had to gather
beans and sweet potatoes. It was hard
to work outdoors. The air was full of
mosquitoes. Thousands of them!

The chief stayed in his hut while others
worked. The mosquitoes found him there.
He couldn't sleep or think.
There was too much buzzing!
The chief was covered
with bites.

Stop | Think | Write

What happens during a <u>harvest</u>?

_____

_____

_____

"Kill the mosquitoes!" the chief said. "I want every last one killed by morning!"

"Why didn't you take my **advice**?" said the grandmother. "We are in this mess because you killed the frogs."

The chief paid no attention to her. Again he told the villagers to kill the mosquitoes.

Stop Think Write

CONCLUSIONS

How do you think people feel about killing the mosquitoes? Why?

_____

_____

_____

People did their best. Still, they couldn't kill every mosquito. There were too many. The next day there were even more.

The chief gave another order. "This time, kill them ALL!" he said.

The people tried again. They did their best. They still couldn't kill all the mosquitoes. There were just too many.

Stop | **Think** | **Write**

How do you think the chief feels when he sees that there are more mosquitoes than ever?

_____

_____

_____

"You should have left those frogs alone," said the grandmother.

"What are you talking about?" said the chief. He was very angry.

"Don't you know that frogs eat mosquitoes? That's why you need frogs!" the grandmother said.

At last, the chief learned his lesson. He found out the hard way that all living things are linked.

Stop | Think | Write

INFER AND PREDICT

How do frogs help people?

_____

_____

_____

Look Back and Respond

1 Is the chief a good listener? How can you tell?

Hint

For clues, look on pages 74, 76, and 78.

_____

_____

2 Why do the people do whatever the chief tells them to do?

Hint

For clues, look on pages 74 and 76.

_____

_____

_____

3 How is the chief's grandmother unlike the other characters in the story?

Hint

For clues, look on pages 74 and 76.

_____

_____

_____

Lesson 9

TARGET VOCABULARY

applause
familiar
jerky
vacant

Storytelling

1 Children in France made a discovery about one hundred years ago. They were in a **vacant** cave. They found pictures on the rock walls. The cave paintings were thousands of years old. The pictures told the story of people who lived there long ago.

What other things can be <u>vacant</u>?

_____

_____

_____

2 In the past, storytellers went from town to town. They shared their stories. Some **familiar** stories were first told long ago.

How do you become <u>familiar</u> with something?

_____

_____

_____

82

3 Storytellers of long ago were fun to watch. Some wore colorful clothes. They sometimes acted out their stories. They made **jerky** movements and funny faces.

What is a word that means the opposite of jerky?

_____

4 Long ago, good storytellers got lots of **applause**. People clap when they hear good stories today, too!

When do we hear applause?

_____

_____

_____

Puppets Around the World

by Lois Grippo

People love puppets! They are a **familiar** toy. Children all around the world love to play with them.

The first puppets may have been made in Egypt. These puppets were simple toys. They were made of wood. Strings made their parts move.

Stop **Think** **Write**

MAIN IDEAS AND DETAILS

What were puppets like long ago in Egypt?

_____

_____

_____

Shadow Puppets

Long ago, people in Southeast Asia made shadow puppets. These puppets were flat. They were made from paper. Each puppet was attached to a stick. Moving the stick made the puppet move.

The puppets were held behind a silk screen. Candles were lit to make shadows.

People sat on the other side of the screen. They could not see the puppets. They could not see the people holding them. They saw large puppet shadows on the silk screen!

Stop **Think** **Write**

CAUSE AND EFFECT

How does a shadow puppet move?

_____

_____

_____

Bunraku Puppets

The Japanese also make special puppets. They are called Bunraku puppets. These puppets are large. They can be as big as a person.

It takes three people to move these puppets. The people appear on stage with the puppet.

The puppet's movements are never **jerky**. People work hard to make the puppets move smoothly.

Stop | **Think** | **Write**

Why aren't the movements of a Bunraku puppet <u>jerky</u>?

_____

_____

_____

Hand Puppets

Did you ever make a sock puppet? A sock puppet is a hand puppet.

There were hand puppets long ago in China. These puppets were not made from socks. They were made from wood. The wood was hollow. A person's hand fit inside.

Stop | **Think** | **Write**

CAUSE AND EFFECT

How does a hand puppet move?

_____

_____

_____

Puppet Theaters

Puppet shows are done on small stages. Sometimes the stage is **vacant**. Often it is filled. There may be trees and homes. There may be hills and farms.

Puppets race across the stage. They peek out of windows. Fans give **applause** when a hero fights a dragon. They boo when the dragon fights back. Puppet shows are fun.

Stop Think Write

Why might you hear <u>applause</u> during a puppet show?

_____

_____

_____

Puppet Shows

What are puppet shows about? Some teach a lesson. Some tell the history of a place. Long ago there were no TVs. There were no newspapers. People learned the news from puppet shows.

So listen closely to puppets! They can be very funny. They can also tell you things you did not know!

Stop | **Think** | **Write**

MAIN IDEAS AND DETAILS

What can you learn from a puppet show?

_____

_____

_____

Make a Sock Puppet

* Ask a grown-up to give you an old sock.

* Draw a face on the foot part of the sock.

* Now, stick your hand in the sock.

* Use your fingers to make a mouth.

* Move the mouth up and down.

* Make your sock say something!

Stop **Think** **Write**

MAIN IDEAS AND DETAILS

How do you make the mouth of a sock puppet?

_____

_____

_____

Look Back and Respond

1 How do people make Bunraku puppets move in lifelike ways?

Hint

For clues, see page 86.

_____

_____

_____

2 How do you think stage scenery helps to bring a puppet show to life?

Hint

For clues, see page 88.

_____

_____

_____

3 What is the difference between a Bunraku puppet and a shadow puppet?

Hint

For clues, see pages 85 and 86.

_____

_____

_____

✓ TARGET VOCABULARY

experiment
genius
invention
laboratory

Inventors

1 An inventor starts with an idea. The inventor does an **experiment** to see if the idea will work.

What <u>experiment</u> could you do to find out which kind of cereal stays crunchy in milk the longest?

_____

_____

_____

2 People may think that an inventor is a **genius** because he or she had an idea that no one else thought of.

What else could someone do that would make you think that person is a <u>genius</u>?

_____

_____

_____

3 If an **invention** is useful, lots of people will want it. The inventor may become famous.

What kind of <u>invention</u> would you like to make?

_____

_____

_____

4 An inventor often works in a **laboratory**. It has equipment to make and test inventions.

What are three things you might find in a <u>laboratory</u>?

_____

_____

_____

Aleck's Big Ideas

by Candyce Norvell

Inventions and Inventors

Think of great inventions of the last one hundred years. The telephone, television, car, and computer are a few of them.

We know how amazing these things are. What about the people who made them? An inventor can be as amazing as his or her **invention**. This is the story of one amazing inventor.

Stop **Think** **Write**

CONCLUSIONS

Why were the telephone and car amazing inventions?

_____

_____

_____

A Boy Named Aleck

In 1847, a boy named Aleck was born in Scotland. He became interested in sound.

One day Aleck got lost. He heard his father calling him from far away. This made Aleck curious about how sound traveled.

As a joke, Aleck and his brothers made a machine. It sounded like a baby crying. Their neighbors thought it was a real baby!

SCOTLAND

Edinburgh

Stop Think Write

CAUSE AND EFFECT

What made Aleck think about how sound traveled?

_____

_____

_____

Early Experiments

Aleck tried new experiments. He even taught his dog to talk! He rubbed its voice box. He moved its jaws. The sounds that came out were like words. Soon the dog could say, "How are you, grandmamma?"

When Aleck was 14, he made a useful machine. Until then, farmers had to take the shell off wheat. Only then could people eat it. The young **genius** made a machine that did this job.

Stop Think Write

Why do you think the author calls Aleck a genius?

_____

_____

_____

Growing Up

Aleck's mother was deaf. Aleck wanted to help her understand the things he said. He wanted to help people who could not hear well.

Aleck went to England to study. He met scientists there. He learned about a new idea called electricity.

Stop Think Write

MAIN IDEAS AND DETAILS

Write a detail that explains why Aleck wanted to help people who couldn't hear well.

_____

_____

_____

Off to America

Later, Aleck moved to the United States. He finished his studies. He then became a teacher. Aleck married Mabel Hubbard. Like Aleck's mother, Mabel could not hear.

Aleck began to work on his biggest invention. It was the telephone. Yes, Aleck was Alexander Graham Bell!

Stop | **Think** | **Write**

SEQUENCE OF EVENTS

What was Aleck's first job after he finished school?

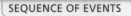

Sending a Message

Aleck had an idea. He wanted to send voice messages over a wire. He and his friend Tom Watson began to try. They worked long hours in their **laboratory**.

During one **experiment**, Aleck hurt himself. Tom was in another room. Aleck said, "Mr. Watson, come here." Tom heard Aleck's voice over the wire! The first telephone message had been sent.

Stop **Think** **Write**

VOCABULARY

What did Aleck and Tom try to do in their laboratory?

_____

_____

_____

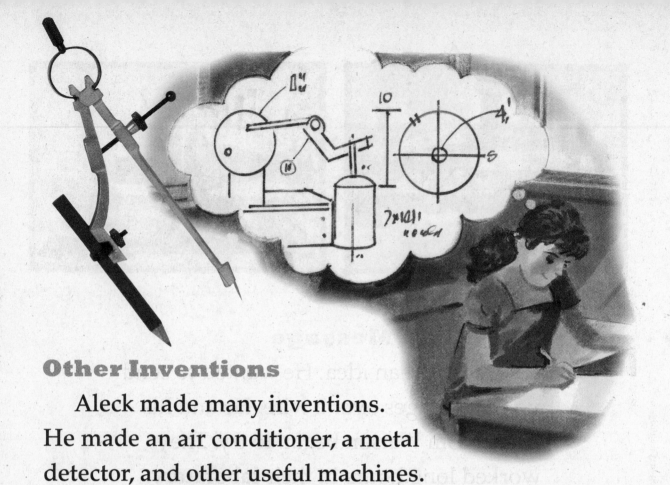

Other Inventions

Aleck made many inventions. He made an air conditioner, a metal detector, and other useful machines.

Alexander Graham Bell once said, "All really big discoveries are the results of thought." Aleck must have thought a lot. He sure made some big discoveries. Every day, other people's thoughts lead to discoveries, too.

Stop | **Think** | **Write**

CAUSE AND EFFECT

How can thoughts lead to big discoveries?

_____

_____

_____

Look Back and Respond

1 **What is the main idea of this story?**

Hint

Think about what every page of the story is mainly about.

_____

_____

_____

2 **Write two details that tell why Aleck was curious about sound.**

Hint

For clues, see pages 95 and 97.

_____

_____

_____

3 **How would you describe Aleck?**

Hint

For clues, see pages 95, 96, and 97.

_____

_____

_____

Athletes

1 It takes skill to be the best in a sport. It takes hard work, too. A top **athlete** practices almost every day.

Who is your favorite <u>athlete</u>? What sport does the person play?

_____

_____

_____

2 Being a good player is not enough. A top athlete must also be a strong **competitor**. He or she must want to be the best!

When were you a <u>competitor</u>? What was the experience like?

_____

_____

_____

3 Some top players become **professional** athletes. They are paid for their work! Lots of people might see these athletes compete.

If you could be a <u>professional</u> athlete, what sport would you play? Why?

_____

_____

_____

4 Fans are important, too. People love going to a game. They love **rooting** for their favorite team. Athletes must love a cheering crowd!

<u>Rooting</u> fans love to cheer. What else might they do?

_____

_____

_____

A Top Golf Player

by Candyce Norvell

How does a star **athlete** get started? Many begin by watching an older brother or sister.

Nancy Lopez was a winning golfer. She learned about golf from her parents. Nancy lived in New Mexico. She watched her parents play golf near their home.

Stop **Think** **Write**

FACT AND OPINION

Nancy Lopez lived in New Mexico. Is this a fact or someone's opinion? How do you know?

_____

_____

_____

Starting Out

Nancy got her first golf clubs when she was eight. Her dad taught her to play.

Nancy's father made a sand trap in their yard. A sand trap is a big hole filled with sand.

Hitting a golf ball out of a sand trap is hard. Nancy wanted to be able to do it. She practiced every day.

Stop **Think** **Write**

CONCLUSIONS

Why do you think Nancy wanted to be able to hit a golf ball out of a sand trap?

_____

_____

_____

Her First Win

Nancy won her first golf contest when she was nine. She won another contest a year later. Young golfers from all over the state played in the event.

When she was twelve, Nancy won another golf contest. Many people were **rooting** for her. They thought that Nancy was a special player.

Stop | **Think** | **Write**

FACT AND OPINION

Reread the first sentence on this page. Is it a fact or an opinion? How do you know?

_____

_____

_____

On the Boys' Team

Nancy continued to play. She practiced all the time. Her high school did not have a golf team for girls. Nancy wanted to compete. She played on the boys' team!

Nancy was a strong **competitor**. The team did well with her help. They were the best team in the state for two years.

After high school, Nancy went to college. Of course, she kept playing golf!

Stop **Think** **Write**

VOCABULARY

How can you tell that Nancy was a strong competitor?

_____

_____

_____

107

A True Golf Star

Nancy decided to make golf her job. She became a **professional** golfer. It was the best thing she ever did!

Nancy did very well. She won nine contests in her first year. In 1978, she had great success. She won five contests in a row. No professional woman golfer had done that before. In 1978 and 1979, she made more money than any other woman golfer.

Nancy was a golf star. She was named "Player of the Year" three times.

Stop | Think | Write

VOCABULARY

What does it mean to be a professional golfer?

_____

_____

_____

You Can't Win Every Time

Top athletes don't always win. Nancy didn't always get a trophy. The U.S. Women's Open is an important event. Nancy never won the contest. She did come in second many times!

Nancy always remembered the words of her father. "You can't win all the time," he said. "As long as you are doing the best you can, that's all that's important."

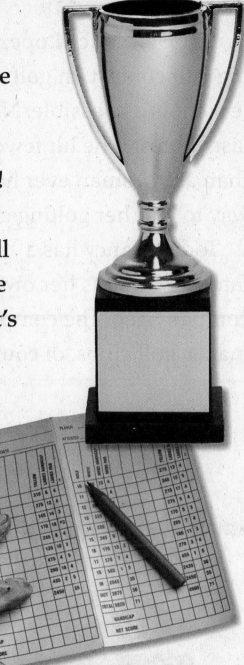

Stop | Think | Write

INFER AND PREDICT

How might Nancy's father's words have helped Nancy to feel good when she did not win?

_____

_____

_____

Nancy's Life Today

In 1997, Nancy Lopez played in her last big golf contest. In golf, players try to use as few shots as possible. Nancy did well in her last contest. She hit fewer shots each day than any woman ever had. It was a great way to end her golfing career.

Today Nancy has a family. She runs her own company, too. The company makes golf clubs, of course!

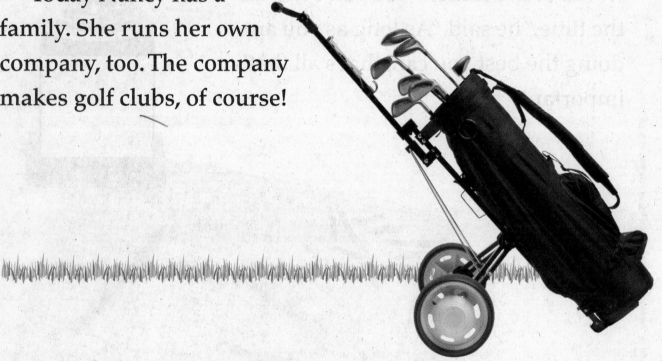

Stop **Think** **Write**

CONCLUSIONS

How do you think Nancy Lopez felt after playing her last golf game?

_____

_____

_____

Look Back and Respond

1 On page 108, the author explains that becoming a professional golfer was the best thing Nancy Lopez ever did. Is this a fact or an opinion? Why?

_____

_____

_____

Hint

Opinions tell what someone thinks or how they feel.

2 What helped Nancy Lopez become a golf star?

_____

_____

_____

Hint

For clues, see pages 104, 105, and 107.

3 Read the last two sentences on page 110. Are they facts or opinions? Why?

_____

_____

_____

Hint

Facts can be proven true.

Making Rainbow Colors

1 Miguel mixed red, blue, and yellow paints. He made new colors. His work was for a science project. Miguel had to **report** his work to the class.

What is a word that has the same meaning as report?

_____

2 Miguel made a **presentation** to his class. He showed how to mix paints to make new colors. Red and yellow made orange. Yellow and blue made green. Red and blue made purple.

Tell about a time when you made a presentation to your class.

_____

_____

_____

3 The teacher gave Miguel a **certificate**. It said that he was a good scientist. Miguel's name was printed in gold letters.

For what kinds of things might a person get a **certificate**?

_____

_____

_____

4 "Your work is very **impressive**," said the teacher. "It is the best science project I've seen all year!" Everyone in class liked it, too.

Tell about an **impressive** thing that you have done. What made it so special?

_____

_____

_____

Mix It Up

by Margaret Maugenest

Last week, there was a science fair. Katie made a **presentation**. She showed what happens when you mix different things. Katie won first prize. She got a special **certificate**.

Now Katie is at home with her brother Zach. They are in the kitchen.

Stop **Think** **Write**

VOCABULARY

What does Katie show at the presentation?

_____

_____

_____

"Let's see what happens when we mix salt and sand," says Katie.

Zach and Katie put salt and sand in a bowl. They mix them up.

"Does the salt change?" asks Katie. "Does the sand change?"

Zach looks in the bowl. "No," he says. "They look the same as before."

"You are right!" says Katie.

Stop **Think** **Write**

STORY STRUCTURE

How do the characters' spoken words help you know what is happening in the story?

_____

_____

_____

"Let's see what happens when we mix salt and water," says Katie.

They put salt and water in a bowl. Zach stirs. Soon the salt disappeared.

"All I see now is clear water," says Zach.

"This mixture is called a solution," says Katie. "The salt dissolved in the water. The salt is still there. We just can't see it."

Stop | **Think** | **Write**

What happens when salt and water are mixed?

_____

_____

_____

"How do you know?" asks Zach.

"I can taste it," says Katie.

"It tastes salty."

Zach tastes the water, too. He makes a funny face. "I don't like salty water."

Zach and Katie laugh.

"Now let's mix sugar and water," says Katie.

Stop Think Write

STORY STRUCTURE

Do Katie and Zach get along well? How do you know?

_____

_____

_____

They clean the bowl. Zach puts in the sugar. Katie adds the water.

"What will happen?" asks Katie. She wants to see if Zach is learning.

"I think the sugar will dissolve," says Zach.

"Right! You got it!" says Katie. "Your work is very **impressive**! How do you think this solution will taste?"

VOCABULARY

Why does Katie think her brother's work is impressive?

_____

_____

_____

_____

Zach takes a taste. "I am happy to **report** that it tastes sweet!" he says.

"I know something else that will dissolve in water," says Zach. He takes out a box of lemonade mix.

"Right again!" says Katie. She gets a pitcher of water and two glasses.

Zach adds the lemonade mix to the water. Katie stirs.

"This solution will taste the best."

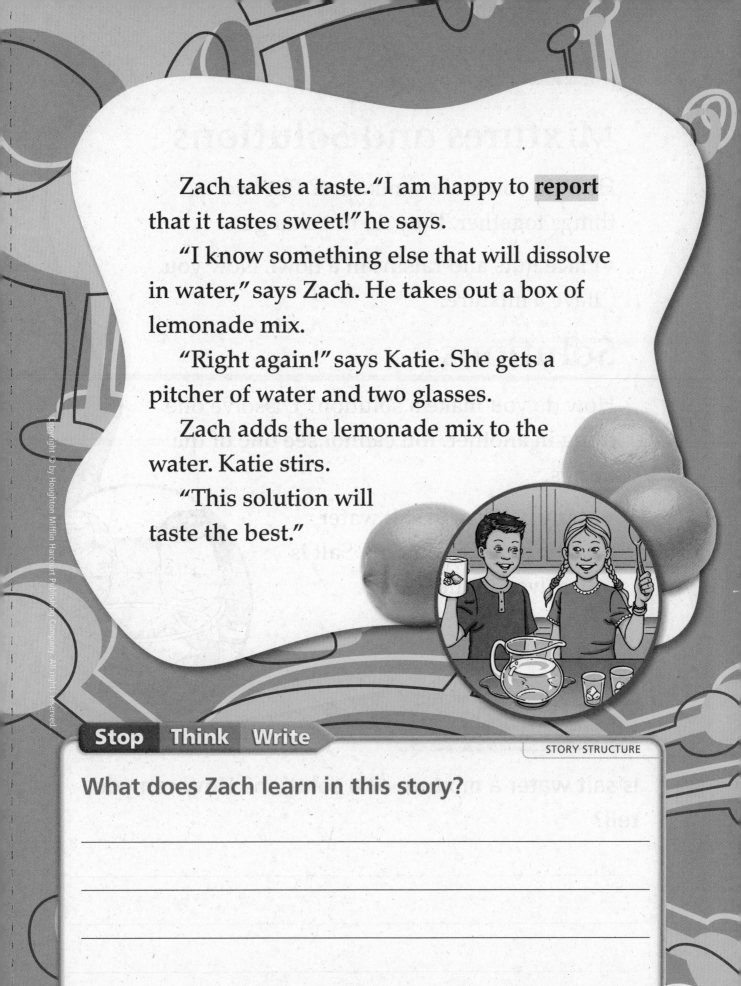

Stop **Think** **Write**

STORY STRUCTURE

What does Zach learn in this story?

_____

_____

_____

Mixtures and Solutions

How do you make a mixture? Put two things together. They do not change.

- Place nuts and raisins in a bowl. Now you have a mixture.

Solutions

How do you make a solution? Dissolve one thing in another. You cannot see one of the things.

- Many fish live in salt water. Salt water is a solution. Salt is dissolved in the water.

Stop **Think** **Write**

MAIN IDEAS AND DETAILS

Is salt water a mixture or a solution? How can you tell?

_____

_____

_____

Look Back and Respond

1 **Where does the story take place?**

Hint

See page 114.

_____

_____

_____

2 **Who is telling the story? One of the characters? A narrator?**

Hint

See page 114.

_____

_____

_____

3 **How can you tell that Katie is good at science?**

Hint

Clues are on every page!

_____

_____

_____

Where the Iroquois Lived

❶ Long ago, the Iroquois lived in what is now New York State. Much of the land had forests and **steep** hills.

Tell about a time when you climbed something steep.

_____

_____

_____

▲ **Trees on steep hills**

❷ The ground in many places was rocky and **rugged**. It could be hard to walk on. The Iroquois traveled by canoe when they could.

Tell about a rugged area where you have been.

_____

_____

_____

3 The Iroquois built longhouses and wigwams. Sometimes they awoke to find **mist** around their homes. The mist went away as the sun rose.

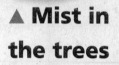

▲ **Mist in the trees**

Write a word that has the same meaning as <u>mist</u>.

_____

_____

_____

4 The Iroquois treated their children **fondly**. Adults rarely punished children or spoke harshly to them.

Tell about someone you treat <u>fondly</u>.

_____

_____

_____

Little Mud-Face

An American Indian Cinderella Tale
retold by Dina McClellan

Long ago, a hunter and his three daughters lived near a lake. Oldest Sister and Middle Sister were mean to their little sister. They made her do all the work.

The little sister had to cook and clean. She carried heavy sticks for the fire. Her face and arms were always dirty. People called her Little Mud-Face.

Stop | **Think** | **Write**

STORY STRUCTURE

Why is the little sister known as Little Mud-Face?

_____

_____

_____

Across the lake was the wigwam of Strong Wind and his sister, Bright Eyes. Bright Eyes loved her brother very much. She could see and hear him. Most other people could not.

One day, Bright Eyes came to the village. "Strong Wind and I are looking for someone to join our happy family," she said. "Only someone who tells the truth may live with us."

Stop **Think** **Write**

COMPARE AND CONTRAST

How is Bright Eyes different from most other people?

_____

_____

_____

Oldest Sister put on her best clothes. She found Bright Eyes by the lake.

"Strong Wind is out fishing," said Bright Eyes. "Can you see him in his canoe?"

"Of course I can," said Oldest Sister.

"What is his bowstring made of?" Bright Eyes asked.

"The hide of a deer," said Oldest Sister.

"Go home now," said Bright Eyes.

Stop | Think | Write

Why does Bright Eyes tell Oldest Sister to go home?

The next day Middle Sister set off. She, too, found Bright Eyes by the lake.

"Do you see my brother near his canoe?"

"Of course," said Middle Sister.

"Then what is his bowstring made of?"

"Braided grass," said Middle Sister.

"Go home now," said Bright Eyes.

Stop | **Think** | **Write**

COMPARE AND CONTRAST

How are Middle Sister's answer and Oldest Sister's answer alike?

The next day Little Mud-Face told her sisters that she would find Bright Eyes and Strong Wind. She would show them that she spoke the truth. Her sisters burst out laughing. Little Mud-Face didn't care.

She started walking around the lake. The land was **rugged**. Little Mud-Face climbed **steep** hills. She walked without pausing to catch her breath.

Stop **Think** **Write**

Is it easy or hard for Little Mud-Face to climb a steep hill?

_____

_____

_____

At last Little Mud-Face reached the lake. The water was covered with **mist**. Bright Eyes was waiting for her.

"Can you see my brother?" she asked.

"Oh, yes," said Little Mud-Face. "How special he is! He has a bowstring made from a rainbow!"

Stop | Think | Write

VOCABULARY

What does Little Mud-Face see through the mist?

_____

_____

_____

"You are right, Little Mud-Face," said Bright Eyes. "Only now you will be Rainbow Star." She led the girl to her wigwam. She cleaned her face and gave her a beautiful robe to wear.

Then Strong Wind came in. He looked at Rainbow Star fondly. "Someone who tells the truth will always be able to see the truth," he said. "From now on, you will be part of our family."

Stop | Think | Write

CONCLUSIONS

Why does Bright Eyes change Little Mud-Face's name to "Rainbow Star"?

_____

_____

_____

Look Back and Respond

1 How is Little Mud-Face different from her sisters?

Hint

Look on pages 124, 129, and 130.

_____

_____

_____

2 How do you know that Little Mud-Face wants very much to show Bright Eyes and Strong Wind that she tells the truth?

Hint

Look on page 128.

_____

_____

_____

3 How is Strong Wind different from the other characters in the story?

Hint

Look on page 125.

_____

_____

_____

✓ **TARGET VOCABULARY**

ability
loyal
lying
partners

Smart Animals

Check the answer.

1 Dolphins have the _____ to talk to each other. They make special sounds that other dolphins understand.

☐ **principal**   ☐ **ability**   ☐ **customers**

2 Humpback whales work as _____ to get food. One whale blows bubbles under a group of fish. The other whale makes sounds to scare the fish. Fish swim to the surface, and whales eat them.

☐ **partners**   ☐ **fans**   ☐ **applause**

3 Dogs spend time _____ around when nobody is home. They know the usual times that people come home. Then they wait by the door or look out the window.

☐ **lying**   ☐ **pausing**   ☐ **tracing**

4 Some monkeys are trained to help people. The monkeys are _____ friends. They are trusty and faithful companions.

☐ **loyal**   ☐ **rugged**   ☐ **electric**

5 What special <u>ability</u> would you like to have? Why?

_____

_____

_____

6 Why is it good to have <u>partners</u> when there is a hard job to do?

_____

_____

_____

Dogs That Help

by Lois Grippo

Who doesn't love their dog? Dogs wait for us to come home. They sleep next to our beds. They bark when they hear strange footsteps. They're always around.

Being a friend is not the only thing a dog can do. For some people, a dog is an important helper. A dog can guide a person who can't see. It can nudge someone who can't hear. A dog can also bring things to a person who can't walk.

Stop   Think   Write

How does the author feel about dogs?
How can you tell?

_____

_____

_____

134

Training

How does a puppy become a helper dog? It must go to school! These schools are special places. Dog trainers work at the schools. They teach dogs how to take care of people with special needs.

A helper dog has a lot to learn. It has to learn the difference between a red light and a green light. It has to learn how to act on a bus and with other animals. It must learn to obey its owner.

A helper dog at work

Stop **Think** **Write**

CAUSE AND EFFECT

Why must a dog go to school before it can become a helper dog?

_____

_____

_____

Getting Started

A helper dog must learn to do special jobs. What jobs must a dog learn? It depends on its owner's needs. Trainers make sure a dog can do the jobs that the person needs.

At last, a trained dog and its new owner meet. They learn how to live as **partners**. The dog helps its owner. The owner cares for the dog.

A helper dog and its owner are partners.

Stop | Think | Write

VOCABULARY

Why does the author say that the dog and its owner are <u>partners</u>?

_____

_____

_____

Seeing-Eye Dogs

Seeing-eye dogs are one kind of helper dog. Their job is to see for a person who cannot.

A seeing-eye dog helps its owner at home and outdoors. The dog leads its owner from place to place. It does not walk too fast or too slow. It protects its owner.

Seeing-eye dogs are smart. They stop when they see a red light. They lead their owner across a street when the light turns green.

Stop **Think** **Write**

MAIN IDEAS AND DETAILS

How do seeing-eye dogs help their owners?

_____

_____

_____

137

Hearing for an Owner

Sounds give information. Many give a warning. Babies cry. Horns honk. Alarms ring. Some people do not have the **ability** to hear. They won't know if there is trouble.

Some dogs are trained to hear for their owners. They are taught to listen for different sounds. The dog may be sleeping or **lying** down. When there is a noise, the dog jumps into action. It runs to its owner. It alerts him or her to the sound.

Stop Think Write

INFER AND PREDICT

If a person can't hear, how might a helper dog warn him or her that someone is at the door?

_____

_____

_____

Heroes

Some people are unable to walk. They can use a wheelchair. However, there are still some things they can't do.

Dogs can be trained to help these people. The dogs are taught to pick things up. They learn to turn lights on and off. They are even trained to push a wheelchair.

Helper dogs are heroes and **loyal** friends. They serve people with special needs. What do they ask for in return? Nothing more than a meal and a pat on the back!

Stop Think Write

VOCABULARY

What kinds of things might a <u>loyal</u> friend do?

_____

_____

_____

Caring for a Dog

Dogs take care of people. People need to know how to take care of dogs.

- Dogs need to run. Be sure to take your dog outside at least two times each day.

- Dogs need to visit the doctor, just like people. They need special shots to help them stay healthy.

- Keep your dog clean. Brush its coat. Give your dog a bath.

- Feed your dog healthy food. Be sure to give your dog plenty of water, too.

- Be as loving and loyal to your dog as your dog is to you!

Stop | **Think** | **Write**

AUTHOR'S PURPOSE

Why does the author tell you how to care for a dog?

_____

_____

_____

Look Back and Respond

1 Do you think the author wrote this story to persuade the reader to get a helper dog? Why or why not?

Hint

Clues you can use are on almost every page. For example, see pages 135 and 137.

_____

_____

2 What are two things a helper dog might do for a person who can't walk?

Hint

For clues, see page 139.

_____

_____

_____

3 What are two ways that a person can take care of a dog?

Hint

For clues, see page 140.

_____

_____

_____

anxiously
ingredients
remarked
tense

A Breakfast Surprise

It was Mom's birthday. Marta and Elena wanted to make breakfast for her. Marta and Elena looked **anxiously** at each other. What could they make?

Dad came into the kitchen. He saw that Marta and Elena looked **tense**. "Mom likes banana pancakes," he said. "First we'll get the **ingredients**."

Dad got eggs, milk, and flour. Marta and Elena mashed up bananas. They mixed everything in a bowl.

Dad cooked the pancakes. Marta and Elena took the pancakes to Mom. She hugged the girls. "This is the best birthday ever," she **remarked**.

1 You would feel good if someone _____ that you did something really well.

2 It is important to get the _____ you need before you start to cook.

3 Friends who are nervous about taking a test might look _____ at each other.

4 Write a word that means the opposite of <u>tense</u>.

_____

5 Write a word that has the same meaning as <u>remarked</u>.

_____

Swedish Meatball Potstickers with Mustard Dipping Sauce

by

Margaret Maugenest

Ava's class was having a food fair. Ava was on the planning team. She came home after the meeting. She threw her bag down. She slumped in a chair. She looked glum.

Stop Think Write

UNDERSTANDING CHARACTERS

How does Ava feel? How can you tell?

_____

_____

_____

"What's the matter?" her mom asked.

"I have to bring food for the fair," said Ava. "The food must tell about my family. I can only bring one dish."

"Make your Chinese potstickers. They're yummy!" Mom **remarked**.

"I don't want to. I make them all the time," said Ava.

Potstickers

Stop | Think | Write

VOCABULARY

How did Ava react when her mom <u>remarked</u> that Ava's potstickers are yummy?

_____

_____

_____

"What about Grandma Ida's Swedish meatballs? She made them in Sweden," said Mom. "She still makes them."

Ava shook her head. "I like the meatballs," she said. "I just don't want to make them for the food fair."

No dish sounded right. Ava looked at her mom **anxiously**. What could Ava bring?

UNDERSTANDING CHARACTERS

How does Ava feel about her mom's ideas?

_____

_____

_____

"What about Dad's side of the family?" Mom said. "They came from Poland. You can make Polish food. Dad's mom was a great cook. I have her recipes."

Ava's mom got a folder. "Let's see. There is Polish stuffed cabbage. There is fish spread. There is mustard dipping sauce, too. These foods are easy to make. They are also very tasty!"

Stop **Think** **Write**

CONCLUSIONS

How can you tell that Ava's mom wants to be helpful?

_____

_____

_____

Ava was not listening. She stared at the floor. Her face had a big frown. She was **tense** and worried.

"What's the matter?" Mom asked.

"I can only bring one dish. I don't have a one-dish story! There is more than one part of me. There's the part that was born in China. Then there's the Swedish part, from you. There's also the Polish part from Dad!"

Stop | **Think** | **Write**

VOCABULARY

Why is Ava <u>tense</u> about bringing one dish?

_____

_____

_____

Mom gave Ava a big hug. "Don't worry. We will find the perfect dish to tell your story," she said.

"A combo dish?" asked Ava.

"Yes. Let's think of something new," said Mom.

Ava's eyes lit up. There was a big smile on her face.

Stop | **Think** | **Write**

UNDERSTANDING CHARACTERS

How does Ava feel now?

_____

_____

_____

"How about Polish stuffed cabbage? I can make it with Chinese soy sauce and Swedish jam," Ava said.

"I'm not sure about the jam," said Mom. "Could we do potstickers with fish spread?"

"Yech!" said Ava. Then she smiled. "I know! I'll make Swedish meatball potstickers with mustard dipping sauce."

"That sounds great!" said Mom. "Let's get the **ingredients** and start!"

Stop | Think | Write

Where can cooks get <u>ingredients</u> they need?

_____

_____

_____

Look Back and Respond

1 Write two words that tell about Ava's mom.

_____

_____

Hint

Clues you can use are on almost every page!

2 What are the different parts of Ava's family background?

_____

_____

_____

Hint

For a clue, see page 148.

3 Why is Ava happy to make a combo dish?

_____

_____

_____

Hint

For a clue, see page 149.

carton
project
recycle
rubbish

Recycling

Check the answer.

1 The United States makes a lot of
_____. We dump it in landfills.
We also burn it.

☐ **rubbish** ☐ **ingredients** ☐ **charts**

2 We can make less waste. We can
_____! We can reuse the materials.
We can use one thing to make
another.

☐ **imagine** ☐ **erupt** ☐ **recycle**

3 You can recycle many things.
Plastic bottles can become chairs.
A _____ can become paper.

☐ **harvest** ☐ **carton** ☐ **tide**

4 You can take things to a recycling center. You can reuse items at home. You can use cans or boxes for a school _____.

☐ **project** ☐ **rubbish** ☐ **advice**

5 Where would you put an empty milk <u>carton</u>?

_____

_____

_____

6 What kinds of things does your school <u>recycle</u>?

_____

_____

_____

Mark's Idea

by Dina McClellan

Jamal's class is learning about recycling. The kids have to do a project. They have to show how they **recycle**.

Jamal wants to make a video. He asks Jen, Paul, and Mark to help.

Jamal writes some notes. He talks them over with his teacher. She likes his ideas. The **project** is a go!

Stop **Think** **Write**

VOCABULARY

Jamal is making a video. What other project about recycling can you think of?

_____

_____

_____

154

Jamal and his friends go to the teachers' room. Mr. Ruiz sees them.

"What's up?" asks Mr. Ruiz.

"We're making a video about recycling," says Paul. "Can we film the trash in the teachers' room?"

Mr. Ruiz smiles. "A video about recycling? That's a great idea!" he says. "Mrs. Hill is here, too. Maybe we can help."

Stop | **Think** | **Write**

AUTHOR'S PURPOSE

Mr. Ruiz says a video about recycling is a great idea. Would the author of this story agree? Explain.

_____

_____

_____

155

Jen has the camera. She zooms in on the **rubbish**. There are four trash bins. One is for plastic. One is for paper. One is for cans. One is for all other trash. Everything is in order.

Jen aims the camera at Mr. Ruiz and Mrs. Hill. They tell about how teachers recycle. When they are done, the kids thank the teachers. Then the kids leave.

"Our video has good facts. Still, I don't think it is much fun," Jamal says.

Stop **Think** **Write**

Why do the teachers put the <u>rubbish</u> in separate bins?

_____

_____

_____

"Let's see how students recycle," Jen says. "That might be fun."

The kids go to the student lunchroom. Jamal has the camera. Jen and Paul smile. "Here is a bin for cans," says Paul. "Inside we see—"

Paul stops. He frowns. "I see plastic bags, bottles, and a milk **carton**!" he says. "They don't belong in there!"

"Stop the camera!" says Jen.

Stop | Think | Write

CAUSE AND EFFECT

Why does Jen say "Stop the camera!"?

_____

_____

_____

"The project is in trouble!" Jen says. "Kids are putting things in the wrong bins. We can't make a video about that!"

"I know what to do!" Mark says. "We don't have to just talk about recycling. We can make a how-to video. We can show how it's done!"

Stop | Think | Write

CAUSE AND EFFECT

Why does Jen think the project is in trouble?

_____

_____

_____

Jen and Paul stand by the bins. Mark turns on the camera.

"Bags and cartons don't go with cans," Paul says. "We can show how to recycle the right way!"

Jen and Paul pick up some trash. They put it in the right bins.

Jamal smiles. "This is more fun," he says. "Our video will be great!"

Stop | Think | Write

Do you think Mark came up with a good idea? Why or why not?

_____

_____

_____

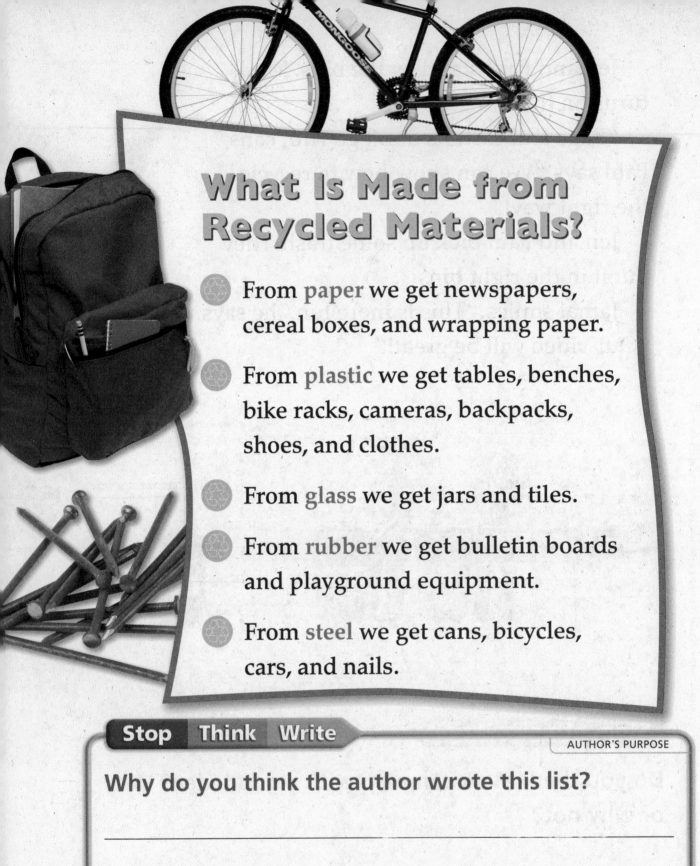

What Is Made from Recycled Materials?

- From **paper** we get newspapers, cereal boxes, and wrapping paper.

- From **plastic** we get tables, benches, bike racks, cameras, backpacks, shoes, and clothes.

- From **glass** we get jars and tiles.

- From **rubber** we get bulletin boards and playground equipment.

- From **steel** we get cans, bicycles, cars, and nails.

Stop **Think** **Write**

Why do you think the author wrote this list?

_____

_____

_____

Look Back and Respond

1 What did you learn about recycling from this story?

_____

_____

_____

Hint

For clues, see pages 156, 157, and 160.

2 Why do the students end up making a how-to video?

_____

_____

_____

Hint

For clues, see pages 157 and 158.

3 Does the author think recycling is important? Explain why or why not.

_____

_____

_____

Hint

Your answer to questions 1 and 2 should help you.

✓ **TARGET VOCABULARY**

buried
evidence
fierce
fossils
remains

Studying Animals from the Past

1 Many animals from the past are not alive today. We can learn about them only from their **remains**.

What types of <u>remains</u> might an animal leave?

_____

_____

_____

2 Experts dig to find the bones of these animals. The bones are **buried** under dirt and rock.

Why must people be careful when digging up <u>buried</u> animal bones?

_____

_____

_____

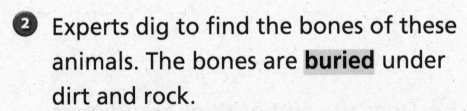

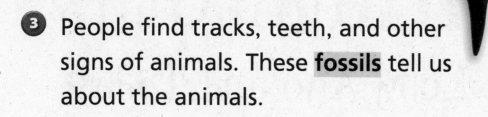

3 People find tracks, teeth, and other signs of animals. These **fossils** tell us about the animals.

What <u>fossils</u> would you like to see?

_____

_____

_____

4 Bones and tracks are not the only **evidence** we have. Cave paintings also tell us about animals from the past.

When you visit a friend's house, what <u>evidence</u> tells you that there is a pet?

_____

_____

_____

5 Some cave paintings show **fierce** beasts. They may be fighting.

Name one <u>fierce</u> animal alive today.

_____

Mammoths
Long Ago and Today

by Candyce Norvell

Our world is full of big animals. Still, no beast on land today is as big as a mammoth. Mammoths lived in the past.

Many mammoths lived during the Ice Age. Much of the land on Earth was frozen. Mammoths had to be tough to stand the cold. They had thick coats of hair. They had body fat to keep them warm. A mammoth weighed about 6,000 pounds.

Stop | **Think** | **Write**

MAIN IDEAS AND DETAILS

Write two details that show that mammoths were large, tough animals.

_____

_____

_____

Plant Eaters

Mammoths did not hunt other animals. They were plant-eaters. They used their trunks to get tree leaves. They pulled plants from the ground, too. They used large, flat teeth to grind up the plants.

A mammoth's trunk had other uses, too. It gave mammoths a great sense of smell. It let them move rocks and trees out of the way. Mammoths may have locked trunks to say hello.

Stop **Think** **Write**

MAIN IDEAS AND DETAILS

How did mammoths use their trunks?

_____

_____

_____

Life in a Mammoth Pack

Mammoths lived together in packs. A pack had several families. Each pack had a leader. The leader was the oldest or strongest mother mammoth.

Mammoths in a pack did not always get along. They could be **fierce**. Sometimes they fought with their tusks. The tusks were about ten feet long. They were tough weapons. The tusks could also dig through snow to get plants.

Stop **Think** **Write**

CONCLUSIONS AND GENERALIZATIONS

Why do you think mammoths roamed in packs?

_____

_____

_____

Mammoths and People

People hunted mammoths. Hunters fought the beasts with stone weapons. They ate the meat. They used the bones to make weapons and tools.

Experts think that hunters prized mammoths. Hunters made paintings of mammoths in caves. The paintings show mammoths as they really looked. This is **evidence** that hunters knew the animals well.

Stop **Think** **Write**

VOCABULARY

What <u>evidence</u> is there that people knew mammoths well?

_____

_____

_____

A Mammoth Find

Mammoths died out long ago. Even so, we know how big they were. In 1974, a large number of bones were found. They were found in a hill in Hot Springs, South Dakota. Workers wanted to put houses on the hill. They brought in big trucks. When they dug, they found giant bones! They were the bones of mammoths. Experts learned a lot from the bones.

◀1

2
▼

Stop **Think** **Write**

CONCLUSIONS AND GENERALIZATIONS

How did people find out how big mammoths were?

_____

_____

_____

3 ▶

4 ▶

Long ago, this land was a deep hole. The hole was full of water and sticky clay. Maybe the animals tried to get a drink and got stuck. They tried to get out, but they could not.

Over time, the spring ran dry. The animal **remains** were **buried**. Their bones were not found for thousands of years. Now Hot Springs is one of the best places to learn about mammoths.

Stop	Think	Write

VOCABULARY

What kind of mammoth <u>remains</u> were found in Hot Springs?

_____

_____

_____

Mammoths in Our World Today

The last mammoth died thousands of years ago. How and why did this happen?

Experts think it got too warm too fast. Plants began to die. Then mammoths didn't have food. Perhaps hunters wiped out the mammoths. We may never know.

We study **fossils** to learn about mammoths. Their story can help us protect animals that live today.

Stop Think Write

CONCLUSIONS AND GENERALIZATIONS

Why doesn't the author tell us why no mammoths are alive today?

_____

_____

_____

Look Back and Respond

1 Why is Hot Springs a good place to learn about mammoths?

Hint

For clues, see pages 168 and 169.

_____

_____

_____

2 What did mammoths eat? How do you think we know that?

Hint

For a clue, see page 165.

_____

_____

3 The author gives two reasons why the mammoths might have died out. Which reason seems more likely to you? Why?

Hint

For clues, see page 170.

_____

_____

_____

Lesson
18

✓ **TARGET VOCABULARY**

absorb
clumps
coverings
store
throughout

Trees

Trees do more than give shade. A tree makes its own food. The leaves make food. They use energy from the sun. Trees have tubes inside them. They carry food to the roots. Roots can **store** food.

Tree leaves come in many shapes and sizes. Some leaves are soft. Other leaves have waxy **coverings**. Some leaves grow in **clumps**. They bunch together.

Trees need water to live and grow. The roots **absorb** water. Water moves **throughout** the tree in its tubes.

1. Some leaves grow in _____, or groups.

2. The _____ of some leaves are waxy.

3. Water travels _____ the tree in its tubes.

4. What is another way to say <u>absorb</u>?

_____

5. What do you <u>store</u> in your room?

_____

_____

_____

The Life of a Hickory Tree

by Dina McClellan

It is fall in the forest. Squirrels are busy. They are looking for nuts. They need to **store** the nuts. They save them to eat in the winter.

This squirrel does not save all the nuts. He eats one now. He cracks the shell. Then he eats the tasty nut.

Stop | Think | Write

TEXT AND GRAPHIC FEATURES

Which part of the text best matches what is happening in the picture?

_____

_____

_____

A Lucky Nut

Another squirrel finds a hickory nut. He hears a noise. He drops the nut and runs away.

The nut hits a stone. It bounces to the ground. Soon, leaves fall on the nut. They hide it.

This is a lucky nut. It will grow into a hickory tree. Most other nuts will not. Squirrels and other animals will eat them.

Stop **Think** **Write**

TEXT AND GRAPHIC FEATURES

Does the heading "A Lucky Nut" tell about the text on this page? How?

_____

_____

_____

Hidden from Sight

Even bears like to eat hickory nuts. They eat them whenever they can.

Bears do not find this hidden nut. The shell of the nut rots. During winter, the nut sinks into the soil.

Animals are looking for food in the forest. Rabbits and mice do not find the nut. It is buried deep in the ground.

Stop | **Think** | **Write**

Why can't the animals find the nut?

_____

_____

_____

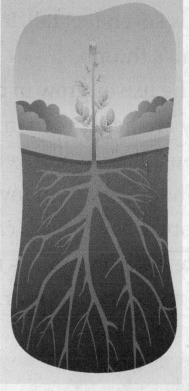

The Seed Sprouts

It is spring in the forest. The seed inside the nut sprouts. It grows roots. They go deep into the ground. The roots **absorb** water from the soil.

The little tree grows. Years pass. The big hickory tree makes more nuts. Most of them never sprout.

Stop | **Think** | **Write**

MAIN IDEAS AND DETAILS

Why are the roots of a tree so important?

_____

_____

_____

177

A Growing Tree

Time passes. After ten years, the tree is seven feet tall. It is as thick as a man's thumb.

The leaves grow in **clumps** of five. They are light green in the summer. In the fall, they turn yellow.

The tree faces many dangers. It can be chopped down. Fires can hurt it. Bugs may make holes in it. Birds may peck the holes and make them bigger.

Stop | **Think** | **Write**

VOCABULARY

Look at the <u>clumps</u> of leaves on the tree. How many leaves are in each clump?

_____

_____

_____

Getting Older

More time passes. After twenty years, the bark is still smooth. Now the tree is thirty years old. Its **coverings** start to split. Each part of the bark is tight in the middle. The edges curve away from the trunk. This makes the tree look shaggy.

After forty years, the first nuts appear. Some of the nuts take root. They might grow into trees. Hickory trees can live for 300 years!

Stop **Think** **Write**

TEXT AND GRAPHIC FEATURES

About how old is the tree in this picture? Look at the bark. Use the text to help you.

_____

_____

_____

The Cycle Goes On

It's fall in the forest. A squirrel comes out. It knows when the hickory tree has nuts. The squirrel looks for them.

Other animals look for nuts, too. Will they find all of the nuts? Will one lucky nut sprout in the spring?

Throughout the forest, trees are growing. Each one is in a different stage of life.

Stop | Think | Write

The picture shows other things that are happening <u>throughout</u> the forest at this time of year. Name three things you see.

_____

_____

_____

Look Back and Respond

1 Which kinds of animals look for hickory nuts?

Hint

For clues, see the sections called "A Lucky Nut" and "Hidden from Sight."

_____

_____

_____

2 How does the hickory tree get water from the soil?

Hint

For clues, see the section that has a heading about sprouting.

_____

_____

_____

3 Look at the trees on the first and last pages of the story. Why do they look similar?

Hint

Think about the story. Read the headings to remind yourself about the tree's life.

_____

_____

_____

horrifying
immediately
mysterious
panicking
within

Two Curious Cats

Lucy brings home a box. She puts the box down. Her cats are curious. They **immediately** jump on the box.

The box is tied with a string. It looks **mysterious**. What is in it?

The cats pull at the string. The box falls from the table. It makes a **horrifying** sound.

The loud sound scares the cats. They quickly run away, **panicking**.

Lucy comes back **within** seconds of hearing the noise. She opens the box. Inside are two cat toys!

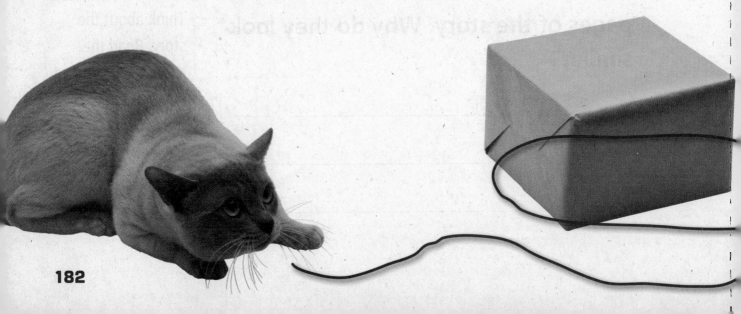

1 The box tied with string looks

_____.

2 Lucy comes back _____
seconds of hearing the noise.

3 The sound makes the cats quickly run
away, _____.

4 Name something you find <u>horrifying</u>.
Explain why.

_____

_____

_____

5 What is your favorite place <u>within</u>
walking distance of your home?

_____

_____

_____

The Case of the Missing Carrots

by Margaret Maugenest

It was a beautiful summer day. Robocat took a walk on the farm. He was happy. His birthday was coming up.

Robocat looked down and saw some paw prints. "Hmm," he said. "This is **mysterious**. I wonder whose paw prints these are."

Robocat followed the paw prints. They led to the vegetable garden.

Stop | **Think** | **Write**

Why are the paw prints <u>mysterious</u> to Robocat?

_____

_____

_____

Robocat walked into the garden. He **immediately** saw some holes. He was shocked and mad.

"Someone has pulled out some carrots," said Robocat. "This is **horrifying**!"

Robocat had to find out who did it. He came up with a clever plan.

Stop | **Think** | **Write**

CAUSE AND EFFECT

Why are there holes in the garden?

_____

_____

_____

That night, Robocat hid in a tree by the garden. "These crooks don't have a chance," he said. "I'll watch this garden all night long. I'll catch them."

Robocat tried to stay awake, but the night was long. The moon rose. Robocat felt cozy in the tree. He got sleepy. **Within** an hour, he fell asleep.

Stop **Think** **Write**

STORY STRUCTURE

Why does Robocat hide in a tree?

_____

_____

_____

Robocat woke up the next morning. He went down to the garden. He saw more holes. More carrots were gone. Robocat filled all the holes.

"I'll catch these crooks yet," he said. "They think they're pretty smart, but Robocat is on the case."

Stop | **Think** | **Write**

CAUSE AND EFFECT

Why are there more holes?

_____

_____

_____

Robocat stood very still in the garden.
He waited for it to get dark.

Night came. The moon shone over the
garden. Robocat heard digging. "I've got
them!" he thought.

He flipped on his lights. He surprised
the animals. They started **panicking**. "Oh,
no, he caught us!" said a voice.

"You should be scared.
Stay right where you are,
you crooks!"

Stop   Think   Write

VOCABULARY

Why are the animals <u>panicking</u>?

_____

_____

_____

Then Robocat went closer. He was shocked. It was Pam Rabbit and the Hoppers.

Pam Rabbit and the Hoppers were his friends. They were not crooks.

"What's going on?" Robocat asked.

"It's a surprise," said Pam Rabbit.

"What do you mean?" asked Robocat.

"Come with us," said Pam Rabbit. The rabbits took Robocat to their secret place.

Stop | **Think** | **Write**

CAUSE AND EFFECT

Why is Robocat shocked?

_____

_____

_____

Robocat saw a big pot. He looked inside it. What he saw made him smile. "Yummy, carrot stew," he said. "That's my favorite!"

"We made it for your birthday," said Pam Rabbit. "We only wanted to take a few carrots at a time. Somehow, we kept nibbling."

Robocat was happy his friends remembered his birthday. "The stew sure smells good," he said. "Let's eat!"

Stop | Think | Write

STORY STRUCTURE

What surprise do the rabbits have for Robocat?

_____

_____

_____

Look Back and Respond

1 **What mystery does Robocat solve?**

Hint

Clues you can use are on almost every page! See pages 185, 186, and 187.

_____

_____

_____

2 **Why doesn't Robocat catch the crooks the first night?**

Hint

For a clue, see page 186.

_____

_____

_____

3 **Why do the rabbits take the carrots?**

Hint

For a clue, see page 190.

_____

_____

_____

✓ **TARGET VOCABULARY**

climate
constant
region
shelter
wilderness

Greenland

1 Greenland is the largest island in the world. The largest **region** of that island is covered in ice. The ice can be up to four feet deep.

What region of the world would you like to visit? Why?

_____

_____

_____

2 The **climate** of Greenland varies. In the north, the temperature is almost always below freezing.

Describe the climate where you live.

_____

_____

_____

3 During the summer, there is
constant daylight.

Write a synonym for <u>constant</u>.

_____

4 Greenland is not all icy **wilderness**.
Nuuk, the capital city, is like many big
cities. It has buildings, traffic jams, and
lots of people.

**Why might people try to keep a
<u>wilderness</u> area the way it is?**

_____

_____

_____

5 Modern-day igloos called space huts
give **shelter** in the coldest areas.

**Name two kinds of <u>shelter</u> in your
town.**

_____

_____

A World of Ice

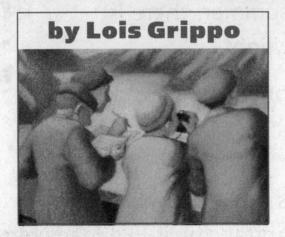

by Lois Grippo

Winter at Sea

It was the winter of 1933. Louise Arner Boyd had been at sea for six weeks. Louise was an explorer. She and her team were making a map. It was of the shore of northeast Greenland. The work was dangerous.

The land was an icy **wilderness**. There was no sign of life.

Stop **Think** **Write**

MAIN IDEAS AND DETAILS

What do you think will be the main idea of this story?

_____

_____

_____

194

The ship moved toward a glacier. Louise stared at the mountain of ice. She took photos. She made notes of everything she saw.

It was very cold. There was no **shelter** from the wind. Louise did not mind. "There is never any hardship in doing what interests you," she said.

Stop | **Think** | **Write**

VOCABULARY

What is the effect of having no <u>shelter</u> from the wind? Explain.

_____

_____

_____

Stuck!

All at once, the ship shook. Louise fell to her knees. There was a loud groan. The ship had run aground.

The captain said, "Reverse the engines!" The crew ran the engines at full speed. The ship didn't move.

They were stuck.

Stop **Think** **Write**

CAUSE AND EFFECT

Why did the ship suddenly shake?

_____

_____

_____

Northeast Greenland was a bad place to be stuck. The **climate** was harsh. In winter, it was the worst. Many cold and hungry explorers had died in this **region**.

There were no other ships nearby. There were no towns or villages. There was no one to save them. Louise and her team would have to save themselves.

Stop | Think | Write

VOCABULARY

Why is northeast Greenland a dangerous region in the winter?

_____

_____

_____

A Dangerous Situation

The tide was getting lower. The water level went down. The crew watched. Their **constant** worry was that the ship would tip over. If it did, they could do nothing.

The ship did not tip over.

When the tide came back in, the ship didn't float off the mud. It was too heavy. It was still stuck.

Stop **Think** **Write**

INFER AND PREDICT

Why would it be terrible if the ship tipped over?

_____

_____

_____

Louise Has a Plan

The crew had to make the ship lighter. The men took three boats off the ship. They unloaded oil and gas. They threw coal overboard.

The tide came in. The ship was still stuck. Louise saw a big iceberg. She had an idea. The crew tied a cable around the iceberg. They would try to pull themselves out of the mud!

Stop **Think** **Write**

MAIN IDEAS AND DETAILS

What did the crew do to make the ship lighter?

_____

_____

_____

The captain ordered the crew to start the engines. The cable was attached to a crank. The engines roared. The crank pulled the cable.

The cable stretched tightly. It began to pull the ship toward the iceberg. The ship lifted off the mud! It was floating again.

Louise's plan had worked. The ship moved safely out to sea.

Stop **Think** **Write**

CAUSE AND EFFECT

How did the crew get the ship out of the mud?

_____

_____

_____

Look Back and Respond

1 **What is the main idea of the story?**

_____

_____

_____

Hint

You'll need to thumb through the whole story.

2 **Why did the crew worry about the tide going down after the ship got stuck?**

_____

_____

_____

Hint

For a clue, see page 198.

3 **Would you like to explore a region like northeast Greenland? Explain.**

_____

_____

_____

Hint

Details about the region are on pages 194, 195, and 197.

narrow
puzzling
scout
surrounded
unaware

Crickets and Grasshoppers

Many people are **unaware** of the way a cricket chirps. It rubs its wings. Its left wing has a **narrow** strip of ridges. Its right wing has a scraper. When the bug rubs those parts together, it chirps.

Crickets chirp faster in warm weather. We may find this **puzzling**. However, it's true!

One kind of grasshopper can swarm. It is the locust. Locusts swarm when they are **surrounded** by other locusts. They fly in a big cloud of insects. They eat everything in their path.

Locusts are destructive. Many areas have a locust **scout**. The scout tells farmers when locusts are getting ready to swarm.

1 Even though it's _____, crickets chirp faster in warm weather.

2 A locust _____ lets farmers know when locusts are about to swarm.

3 Some people are _____ of how a cricket chirps.

4 Name two animals that can fit through <u>narrow</u> spaces.

_____

_____

5 What are some things you are <u>surrounded</u> by at school? Explain.

_____

_____

_____

Gus and Greta

by Mia Lewis

Once there was a cricket. His name was Gus. He lived in a cage. He had plenty to eat. A boy named Juan fed him grass and leaves. Still, Gus had a problem. He was bored!

"Here I am in this boring cage," he said. "There is nothing to do. There is no one to talk to. No crickets, that is."

Stop **Think** **Write**

STORY STRUCTURE

What problem does Gus have?

_____

_____

_____

Gus was **puzzling** to Juan. Juan fed him good food. The cricket should have been happy! The little guy did not seem happy. He sat all day long in one spot. He stared out the window.

Juan started to open the cage. He was going to take a closer look at Gus. Then the phone rang. Juan ran to get it. He was **unaware** that he hadn't closed the cage. Gus crawled under a leaf. He wanted to take a nap.

Stop Think Write

Why does Juan leave Gus's cage open?

_____

_____

_____

Gus fell asleep. He felt a tap.

"Hey! Wake up!" said a voice. "I'm Greta. Your cage was open. I slipped in. Now we can both slip out! Come quickly before the boy sees us!"

Gus did not know this cricket. Still, he was happy to go. Life was too boring in his cage. The opening was **narrow**. Greta and Gus squeezed through.

Stop | Think | Write

STORY STRUCTURE

What does Greta help Gus to do?

_____

_____

_____

Gus was scared to be out of the cage. "Is it safe?" he asked.

"You stay here," said Greta. "I'll be a **scout**. I'll see if the coast is clear."

Greta hopped to an open window. All was clear. Gus hopped over to her. They jumped out the window!

Stop **Think** **Write**

Why does Greta act as the <u>scout</u>, and not Gus?

_____

_____

_____

Gus ran to keep up with Greta. They hopped across the garden. They passed a line of ants. They passed a big hose. It was like a tall tower. Gus stayed close to Greta.

"Listen!" Greta said. "Do you hear that sound? That's where we're going!"

Gus heard a lovely chirping. What was making the sound?

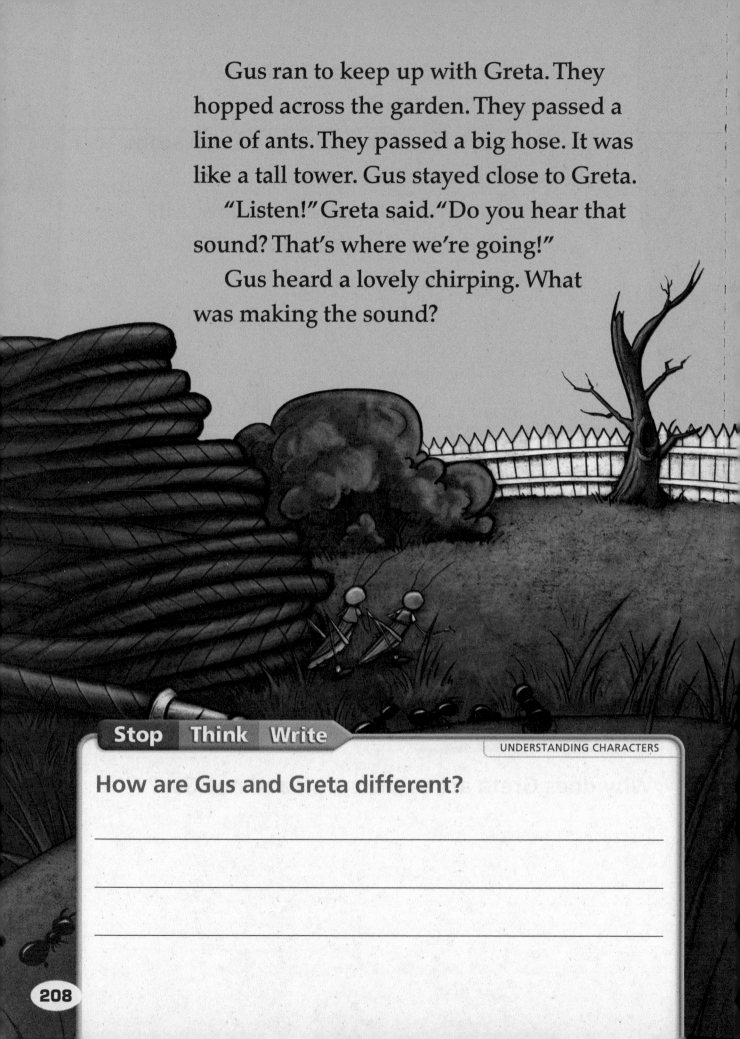

Stop **Think** **Write**

How are Gus and Greta different?

_____

_____

_____

Greta led Gus to the end of the garden. Near the fence was a tree. Greta hopped up the trunk. Gus hopped up after her. Greta jumped into a big hole in the trunk.

"My goodness," said Gus. He felt nervous. "What should I do?"

Then he heard the chirping again. It was coming from the hole!

Stop **Think** **Write**

STORY STRUCTURE

Why doesn't Gus follow Greta into the hole right away?

_____

_____

_____

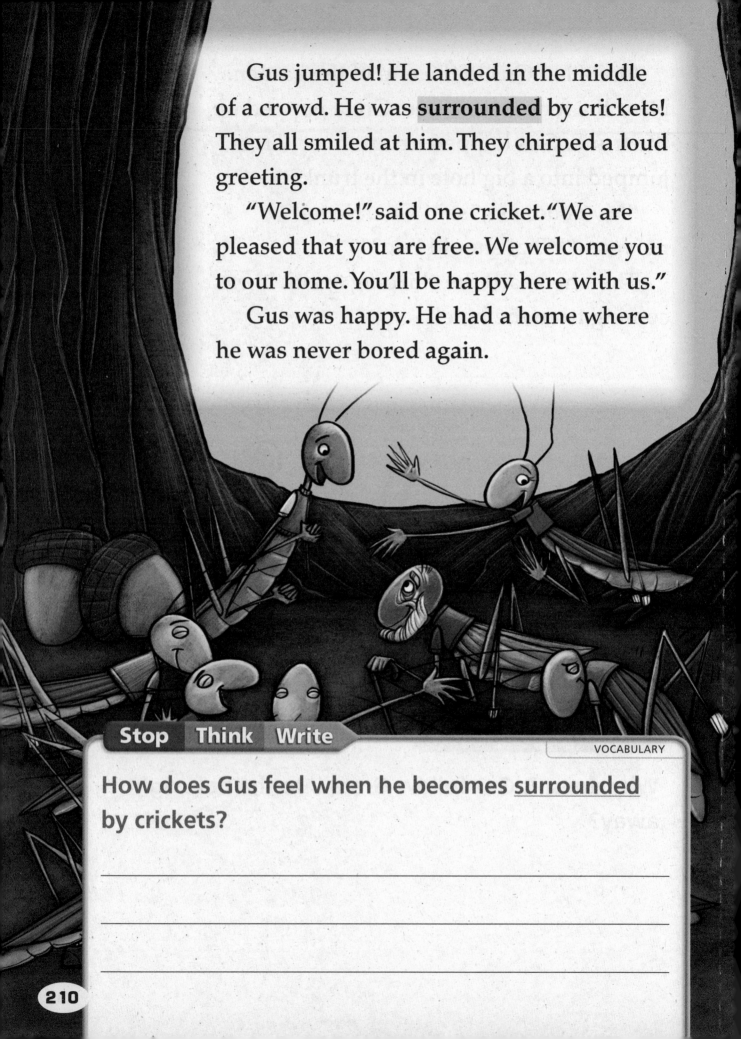

Gus jumped! He landed in the middle of a crowd. He was **surrounded** by crickets! They all smiled at him. They chirped a loud greeting.

"Welcome!" said one cricket. "We are pleased that you are free. We welcome you to our home. You'll be happy here with us."

Gus was happy. He had a home where he was never bored again.

Stop **Think** **Write**

How does Gus feel when he becomes <u>surrounded</u> by crickets?

_____

_____

_____

Look Back and Respond

1 **What is the setting at the beginning of the story?**

Hint

For clues, see pages 204 and 205.

_____

_____

2 **Why does Gus follow Greta?**

Hint

For clues, see pages 204, 205, and 206.

_____

_____

3 **Tell the plot of this story in one or two sentences.**

Hint

Tell just the most important things that happen.

_____

_____

chilly
landscape
migrate
plenty
survival

Birds in Summer and Winter

1 All animals need food to live. They also need water for their **survival**.

Why is <u>survival</u> easier in spring and summer?

_____

_____

_____

2 There is **plenty** of food in spring and summer. There is not as much food in winter.

Do you have <u>plenty</u> of space in your backpack for all your books?

_____

_____

_____

3 The weather gets cold in winter. Many birds **migrate**. They go to warmer places.

What word has almost the same meaning as migrate?

_____

4 Ducks, geese, and swans fly south. You can see flocks of birds. They fly over the **landscape**.

Think of where you live. What things can you see in the landscape?

_____

_____

_____

5 In the spring, the weather gets warm. It is not so **chilly**. The birds come back.

What is the opposite of chilly?

_____

Snow Petrels

by Margaret Maugenest

Winter in Antarctica

Antarctica is a **chilly** place at the South Pole. It is the coldest place on Earth. Ice covers the ground all year.

Winter in Antarctica begins in June. The days are very short. There is no light in the sky. It is dark all of the time. Few animals live in Antarctica. There is little food. **Survival** is very hard.

Stop **Think** **Write**

VOCABULARY

What detail in the first paragraph tells how <u>chilly</u> it is in Antarctica?

_____

_____

_____

Warming Up

Spring comes in September. The days get longer. The sun shines into the sea. The sea becomes rich with small plants.

More animals come. Little animals called krill swim by. They eat the plants. Bigger fish come. They eat the plants and the krill.

Other animals come. There is **plenty** of food. Seals, whales, and birds hunt smaller animals. They eat krill and fish.

Sea plants

Small fish

Stop   Think   Write

COMPARE AND CONTRAST

How are the days in spring different from the days in winter?

_____

_____

_____

215

Summer Days

Summer begins in December. Whales **migrate** to the Antarctic waters. They feed on the krill.

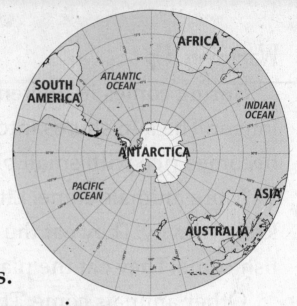

Now the sea is full of life. Flying birds come. They make nests on the shore.

Some of these birds are petrels. Petrels are like sea gulls. Their strong wings let them fly far from land. Their thick coats keep them warm. Most birds can't smell. Petrels can. They sniff out a meal.

Stop | **Think** | **Write**

VOCABULARY

Why do animals migrate to Antarctica in December?

_____

_____

_____

Robin

Snow petrel

Snow Petrel Facts

Snow petrels are much smaller than other petrels. They are about the size of robins. Their feathers are white. They blend in with the snowy **landscape**. Only their bills, eyes, and feet are dark. When they fly, they flutter like bats.

Stop **Think** **Write**

MAIN IDEAS AND DETAILS

What part or parts of a snow petrel are the color of snow?

Habits of Snow Petrels

Snow petrels are shy. If bothered, they may just fly away. If something gets too close, they have a trick. They spit out a liquid that smells very bad!

These birds fly low over the sea to find food. When they see their dinner, they dive into the water to catch it. Some birds roll in dust to clean their feathers. Snow petrels roll in the snow. That is how they clean up after they hunt.

Stop | Think | Write

COMPARE AND CONTRAST

Think about how some birds clean their feathers. What is different about how snow petrels do it?

_____

_____

_____

Petrel Families

A snow petrel finds a partner. Then the pair makes a nest. Like all birds, snow petrels look for a spot safe from other animals. Petrels make their nests in holes on rocky cliffs.

Most birds make their nests with leaves and grass. It's hard to find leaves or grass in Antarctica. Snow petrels line their nests with small pebbles.

The female lays one egg. Six weeks later, the chick hatches. In seven weeks it will fly away. It may live up to twenty years.

Stop **Think** **Write**

COMPARE AND CONTRAST

How is a snow petrel nest different from the nest of most birds?

_____

_____

_____

The North Pole (Arctic) and the South Pole (Antarctic)

- The North Pole is at the top of Earth. The South Pole is at the bottom of Earth.

- The North Pole and the South Pole stay dark during the winter. They stay light during the summer.

- The North Pole and the South Pole are very cold places.

North Pole

South Pole

When Different Seasons Begin in the North and South Poles				
	Winter	**Spring**	**Summer**	**Fall**
North Pole	December	March	June	September
South Pole	June	September	December	March

Stop **Think** **Write**

COMPARE AND CONTRAST

Write one way the North Pole and South Pole are alike. Write one way they are different.

_____

_____

_____

Look Back and Respond

1 How is life in Antarctica different in winter than in spring and summer?

_____

_____

_____

Hint

For clues, see pages 214, 215, and 216.

2 Birds, seals, and whales come to Antarctica in the summer. Why don't they live there in the winter?

_____

_____

_____

Hint

For clues, see pages 214 and 220.

3 How is the snow petrel different from other birds?

_____

_____

_____

Hint

For clues, see pages 216, 217, 218, and 219.

✓ **TARGET VOCABULARY**

currently
loaded
managed
pleasure
terror

Science Fiction

Science fiction stories are about things that **currently** cannot happen. People may be **loaded** onto a spaceship. They may be flown to another planet. They may travel through time.

Writers have **managed** to make these ideas seem real. We can imagine different worlds through their stories.

We read these stories for **pleasure**. It's fun to think about different places and times. We even enjoy feeling **terror** if there are evil space creatures. That can be fun, too!

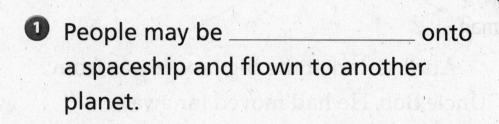

1. People may be _____ onto a spaceship and flown to another planet.

2. We may feel _____ when we read about evil space creatures.

3. We read science fiction stories for _____.

4. What are you <u>currently</u> studying in social studies?

   _____

   _____

   _____

5. What is the most difficult thing that you have <u>managed</u> to do this year?

   _____

   _____

   _____

Dog of the Future

by Estelle Kleinman

April stared at the big box. It was from Uncle Bob. He had moved far away in 3045. That was five years ago. He never forgot her birthday.

She opened the box. Her eyes opened wide. Uncle Bob had made a robot dog for her!

A note was in the box. April read it. She grabbed the robot dog. "I'll call you Joe," she said. She **loaded** Joe into her speedboat. She headed for Paco's place.

Stop | **Think** | **Write**

What does April do right before getting into her boat?

_____

_____

_____

Paco didn't think much of Joe. "A bunch of tin and screws isn't the same as a real dog," he said.

"Oink!" complained Joe.

"I guess Uncle Bob still needs to work some things out. Can you come on my boat?" asked April. "Then I can show you why Joe is so great."

"**Currently**, I have no other plans." Paco said. He hopped on the boat.

Stop | **Think** | **Write**

CONCLUSIONS AND GENERALIZATIONS

What part of Joe does Uncle Bob need to work on?

_____

_____

_____

225

"Let's take a trip," said April. "I'll show you why Joe is a good dog."

Joe took the wheel. He steered the boat away from the dock.

"Can he really control the boat?" Paco asked.

"Yes," answered April. "Uncle Bob says I just have to punch in where we want to go." Joe had a keyboard on his back. April typed in "Tower Cliffs."

Stop **Think** **Write**

SEQUENCE OF EVENTS

After Joe steers the boat away, what does April do?

_____

_____

_____

The water began to get very rough.

"Joe, I'm getting scared!" Paco cried with **terror** in his voice.

Joe slowed the boat to a crawl. A few minutes later, the boat stopped.

"That's not Tower Cliffs," Paco noted. "It's Rocky Bluff."

"Oink! Joe made a mistake," said Joe.

Stop | Think | Write

Why is there <u>terror</u> in Paco's voice?

_____

_____

_____

"I'll tell Uncle Bob about the problems. I'm sure he can fix Joe," said April.

Joe tried again. This time he **managed** to get to Tower Cliffs. They all stepped onto the beach.

"Just watch the fancy tricks Joe can do," April said. "He can throw the ball and catch it!"

Paco wasn't impressed. "I prefer real dogs. They're full of surprises."

Stop **Think** **Write**

COMPARE AND CONTRAST

How are April and Paco different?

_____

_____

_____

Joe picked up the ball. "Should Joe throw right or left? Fast or slow?"

"How disappointing!" said Paco. "This takes the fun out of playing ball."

"Just throw the ball!" April called.

Joe threw the ball. Then he ran to make the perfect catch.

April stopped and looked around. "What's that noise?"

Paco said, "I hear yelling and barking!"

Stop | Think | Write

UNDERSTANDING CHARACTERS

Why is Paco disappointed with Joe?

_____

_____

_____

A brown dog ran up to April and Paco. His owner, Tina, was not far behind.

April told Tina, "We were just playing ball with my robot dog."

Tina asked if her dog Max could play. Paco threw the ball. Max ran after it. He dropped the ball at Paco's feet. Before Paco could get the ball, Joe picked it up. He threw it.

Tina laughed. "Real or robot, these two dogs are a **pleasure** to watch."

Stop **Think** **Write**

Why do you think that Tina takes pleasure in watching the dogs?

_____

_____

_____

Look Back and Respond

1 **What happens at the beginning of the story?**

Hint

For a clue, see page 224.

_____

_____

_____

2 **After Paco hops in the boat, what does Joe do?**

Hint

For clues, see pages 225 and 226.

_____

_____

_____

3 **How does the story end?**

Hint

For a clue, see page 230.

_____

_____

_____

✓ **TARGET VOCABULARY**

**aboard
anchor
bay
spotted
voyage**

Sea Travel

1 People have always traveled across water. Today, we can fly a plane over the sea. Long ago, a sea **voyage** usually took place in a ship.

What do people use to make a voyage over land?

_____

_____

_____

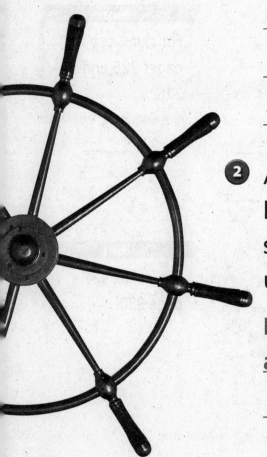

2 A ship had a crew **aboard**. The crew had to know many things. They studied how the winds moved. They used the sails to catch the wind.

How do you think you would feel aboard a ship?

_____

_____

_____

3 Ships sailed on open waters. Weeks might pass before the crew **spotted** land.

What is another way to say spotted?

_____

4 They usually looked for a **bay**. Land around the bay kept the ship safe from winds and waves.

Why is a bay a safe place for a ship?

_____

_____

_____

5 The crew would drop an **anchor** into the water. It held the ship in place. The crew rowed to land in a small boat.

Why must an anchor be heavy?

_____

_____

_____

To the South Seas

by Margaret Maugenest

In the late 1700s, there were few maps of the South Seas. Scientists in England wanted to know about the land in the South Pacific. Was there a huge continent there? Some people thought there was. They asked Captain James Cook to go find out.

Stop Think Write

What clues on this page tell you that this story contains facts?

_____

_____

_____

An ocean trip was long. It was hard. There were many dangers. The seas could get stormy. Pirates could attack. A fire could break out. There was no way to get help.

Cook got ready for the **voyage**. They filled the ship with supplies. They took fresh water. They took food. They had a goat for milk.

Cook's Voyage

Stop | **Think** | **Write**

AUTHOR'S PURPOSE

Look at the picture. What does it show you?

_____

_____

_____

Setting Sail

Ninety-five crew members were **aboard**. Each person on the ship had a certain job.

The ship left England in 1789. It sailed west. It crossed the Atlantic. It went around the tip of South America. A huge storm came up! Five of the men died.

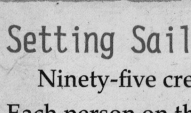

Stop **Think** **Write**

STORY STRUCTURE

What happened as the ship went around the tip of South America?

_____

_____

_____

236

The ship sailed for ten more weeks. The men started to run out of food. They did not want to starve. They caught fish to stay alive.

They went through the South Pacific. The men finally **spotted** Tahiti. The men were happy. They could not wait to reach the island. They had been at sea for eight months.

Stop **Think** **Write**

VOCABULARY

How long had the men been at sea when they <u>spotted</u> Tahiti?

_____

_____

_____

Land, Ho!

The ship sailed into a **bay**. The crew dropped the **anchor**. This held the ship in place. Then the crew got into a smaller boat. They rowed to land.

At first, the people who lived there were uneasy. They did not know Captain Cook. They wanted to know what Cook wanted. Soon they became friendly.

Stop **Think** **Write**

Why was the <u>anchor</u> dropped when the ship was near land?

_____

_____

_____

Cook stayed in Tahiti for three months. He made a map of the island. His scientists studied the plants there.

Then Cook sailed on. He explored the South Seas more. He looked for a huge continent. He did not find one. Cook did see a smaller continent. It was Australia. Mapmakers now had to make new maps.

Stop **Think** **Write**

SEQUENCE OF EVENTS

What did Cook do after he left Tahiti?

_____

_____

_____

Cook's Maps

Cook made two more sea trips. He changed old maps. He showed places where he had been. He made many new maps. He made a map of the west coast of North America. It went all the way up to Alaska.

Other explorers used his maps. There used to be many different maps of the same land. Cook's maps made travel less confusing. They also made travel safer.

Stop Think Write

CONCLUSIONS

How did Captain Cook help future explorers?

_____

_____

_____

Look Back and Respond

1 **Why did Cook set sail in 1789?**

Hint

For clues, see pages 234 and 236.

_____

_____

_____

2 **How did the people of Tahiti act towards Captain Cook and his crew ?**

Hint

For clues, see page 238.

_____

_____

_____

3 **What did Captain Cook find out about the continent in the South Seas?**

Hint

For a clue, see page 239.

_____

_____

_____

Outdoor Gear

✓ TARGET VOCABULARY

altitude
avalanches
equipment
increases
slopes

① Mountain climbing is a fun sport. Still, it is important to stay safe. Special gear can help climbers in **avalanches**. A long red cord can mark where a climber is trapped under snow.

What other equipment might help a climber in <u>avalanches</u>?

_____

_____

_____

② The sun can be strong at a high **altitude**. You should wear sunscreen to protect your skin.

Have you ever been at a high <u>altitude</u>? What was it like?

_____

_____

_____

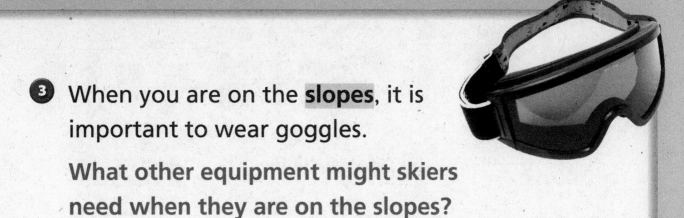

3 When you are on the **slopes**, it is important to wear goggles.

What other equipment might skiers need when they are on the <u>slopes</u>?

_____

_____

_____

4 Danger **increases** when you do not have the right safety gear.

What <u>increases</u> your chance of getting a good seat at the movies?

_____

_____

_____

5 One piece of **equipment** that helps a climber find his way is a compass.

Name another piece of <u>equipment</u> a climber could use.

_____

Ski Patrol

by Dina McClellan

The men and women of the ski patrol do important work. They risk their lives to keep people safe.

Blizzards

One job of the ski patrol is to help people in blizzards. Blizzards are bad news for skiers. Strong winds can make skiers fall. Ice and snow make it hard for them to see.

Stop **Think** **Write**

TEXT AND GRAPHIC FEATURES

What is the title of this text?

_____

_____

_____

Avalanches

Avalanches happen when a huge chunk of snow slides down a mountain. People can get trapped inside the snow. They need help to get out.

The ski patrol has dogs. They are trained to find people in the snow. First the dogs find where the people are trapped. Then the ski patrol works fast to dig them out.

Stop | **Think** | **Write**

VOCABULARY

How do you think dogs find people in avalanches?

_____

_____

_____

What happens after a person is dug out? The person may be hurt. The ski patrol is trained to do first aid. They give care on the spot.

Some hurt people need even more help. The ski patrol moves these people off the **slopes**. They use helicopters, sleds, and snowmobiles. They get people to a hospital fast!

Stop Think Write

VOCABULARY

Why can't ambulances go on the <u>slopes</u>?

_____

_____

_____

Snow Gear

The men and women of the ski patrol have special **equipment**. They always wear bright clothing. That way people can recognize them.

Skiers should wear bright clothing, too. If they are lost, bright clothing **increases** their chances of being seen. Then they can get help.

Stop | **Think** | **Write**

CONCLUSIONS AND GENERALIZATIONS

What colors are most easily seen in snow?

_____

_____

_____

Ski Patrol Schedule

Mornings are busy for the ski patrol. They check mountain trails. They mark spots that aren't safe. They warn people about dangers that may occur at such a high **altitude**.

During the day, the ski patrol checks trails again. They look to see if anyone is lost, hurt, or trapped.

Stop **Think** **Write**

MAIN IDEAS AND DETAILS

Why does the ski patrol check mountain trails?

_____

_____

_____

248

The ski patrol works long hours. They must be sure that every skier is off the mountain at the end of the day. They make sure everyone is safe. Only then can they rest!

Stop | **Think** | **Write**

INFER AND PREDICT

How do you think the men and women of the ski patrol feel at the end the day?

_____

_____

_____

Things a Skier Might Need

Large orange plastic bag

This can attract attention. You can also climb into it to stay dry.

Ski helmet

This can protect your head while you ski.

Whistle

This can attract attention. Three blasts is a signal for help.

Compass

This helps you find your way if you are lost.

Goggles

These are important for seeing in the bright snow.

Fleece vest

This helps you stay warm.

Stop   Think   Write

TEXT AND GRAPHIC FEATURES

Which two items on the list have the same purpose?

_____

_____

_____

Look Back and Respond

1 What do headings in this text tell you?

_____

_____

_____

Hint

To answer this question, look on pages 244, 245, 247, and 248.

2 What is page 245 mostly about?

_____

_____

_____

Hint

Look at the heading.

3 How does the ski patrol help people who are hurt?

_____

_____

_____

Hint

For a clue, see page 246.

Lesson 26

✓ TARGET VOCABULARY

ancient
announced
collect
loveliest
proud

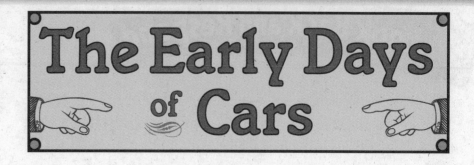

The Early Days of Cars

1 Owning a car was rare in 1900. Most people used horses to travel. Few people could buy a car. They were **proud** of the new machines.

What is something you are <u>proud</u> of?

_____

_____

_____

2 Today, the first cars seem like **ancient** machines. They did not go fast. They often broke down.

What is something else people used to use that seems <u>ancient</u> to you now?

_____

_____

_____

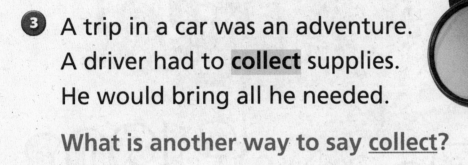

3 A trip in a car was an adventure.
A driver had to **collect** supplies.
He would bring all he needed.

What is another way to say <u>collect</u>?

_____

4 Even the **loveliest** weather can change.
Rain was a problem. Drivers got wet.

What is the <u>loveliest</u> thing you've seen?

_____

_____

5 Drivers often brought a friend along.
The friend **announced** any dangers.

What is something your principal <u>announced</u>?

_____

_____

The Race of 1903

by Dina McClellan

The first cars were made over 100 years ago. They weren't called cars. They were called autos.

Most people had never seen an auto. Automakers wanted to show off their new machines. They **announced** that they would hold a race.

Stop Think Write

VOCABULARY

How do you think people felt when automakers <u>announced</u> they would hold a race?

_____

_____

_____

A Race Across the Country

The Great Race took place in 1903. The race was across the whole country. It started in San Francisco. It ended in New York.

The cars in the race only had front seats. They had no windshields. They went only thirty miles per hour. People thought the cars were amazing. Today these cars seem like **ancient** machines.

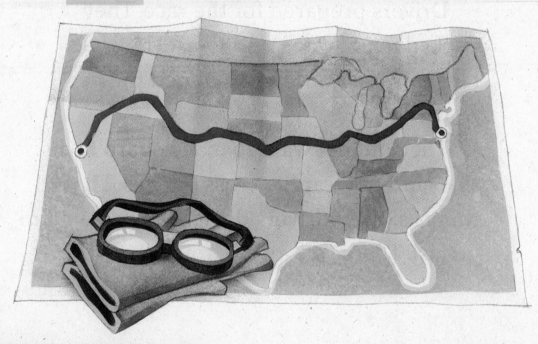

Stop **Think** **Write**

VOCABULARY

Why do early cars seem <u>ancient</u> today?

_____

_____

_____

Drivers prepared for the race. They packed food, water, and tools. They had tarps for the rain. They planned the best route.

They did not want to make sharp turns. They did not want to cross ditches. Those things slowed drivers down. They wanted to go fast. There was a prize for the winner.

Stop **Think** **Write**

MAIN IDEAS AND DETAILS

What did drivers do to prepare for the long trip?

_____

_____

_____

They're Off!

The race began on one of the **loveliest** mornings in June. Crowds lined the streets of San Francisco. Bands played. The mayor gave a speech. The cars lined up. They were ready to go.

Then the cars took off! Some went off the roads. This was dangerous. A car could run into a ditch. It might break down.

Stop **Think** **Write**

MAIN IDEAS AND DETAILS

What took place before the start of the race?

_____

_____

_____

Rough Roads

Sometimes roads were bad. Then the drivers had to slow down. They sped up when the roads were good. The cars made the air dusty. The cars did not have windshields. Each person in the car had to wear goggles.

Cars often got flat tires. Their engines broke. Then the cars needed to be fixed. Drivers fell behind in the race.

Stop · Think · Write

MAIN IDEAS AND DETAILS

What made the trip difficult? Name some things that could go wrong.

_____

_____

_____

Along the Way

People came to watch. They stood next to the road. They cheered as the cars drove by.

Some drivers tried to **collect** money. They did this by giving people rides in their cars. Then they bought more supplies for the trip.

Stop | **Think** | **Write**

INFER AND PREDICT

Why would people pay money just to ride in a car?

_____

_____

_____

Reaching the Finish

The race lasted for two months. At last the drivers reached New York. They were covered in mud. They were tired. Still, they were **proud**.

The Great Race of 1903 was big news. It made people think that the auto was more than a neat machine. It was a great way to travel.

Stop **Think** **Write**

INFER AND PREDICT

What do you think happened as a result of the car's new popularity?

_____

_____

_____

Look Back and Respond

1 How were cars of the past different from the cars of today?

Hint

For clues, see pages 255 and 258.

_____

_____

_____

2 What could make drivers lose time in the race?

Hint

For clues, see pages 256, 257, and 258.

_____

_____

_____

3 Why was the race important?

Hint

For clues, see pages 254 and 260.

_____

_____

_____

experiment
familiar
invention
research
scientific

Machines with Magnets

Magnets are found in many machines. Some machines are **familiar**. They are things you know. A doorbell has magnets. An **invention** such as a computer has magnets. A hair dryer has magnets.

People use a **scientific** process to make a new machine. They learn the science of how magnets work. They do **research**. They think of how to use magnets to make something new.

Will the new machine work? Scientists do an **experiment**. They test the machine. They see if it works well. If it does, then people can use it!

1. A new _____ might be

   a machine that uses magnets.

2. Scientists follow a

   _____ process to make

   a new machine.

3. Machines you see every day are

   _____ to you.

4. Scientists do _____ to

   learn about something. They learn facts

   that help them make something new.

5. Scientists try out inventions. They

   might do an _____ to

   see if a new invention works.

The Boy Who Made the TV

by Cate Foley

Have you heard of Philo T. Farnsworth? If not, don't worry. Many people are not **familiar** with him. Philo Farnsworth made a popular **invention**. He made the modern television. He was just fourteen years old when he got the idea.

| Stop | Think | Write |

VOCABULARY

What <u>invention</u> did Philo Farnsworth make?

_____

_____

_____

264

Farm Boy

Philo was born in Utah in 1906. He helped work on his family's farm.

Philo's family moved to another farm. It was in Idaho. Philo was a teenager. He found something in the attic. He found **scientific** magazines. They changed his life.

Stop | Think | Write

INFER AND PREDICT

Predict how the magazines changed Philo's life.

_____

_____

_____

Philo's Idea

Philo read the magazines. He learned about something called electrons. He read about a new idea. People wanted to use electrons to send pictures through the air.

One day Philo was plowing a field. He thought about electrons. He wondered if they could go back and forth like the plow. Maybe electrons could read pictures line by line! This was a new idea.

Stop | **Think** | **Write**

CAUSE AND EFFECT

How did plowing a field help Philo get a new idea about electrons?

_____

_____

_____

Television was different then. One kind showed a picture on a wall. Philo had a new idea. He wanted to make an electron tube. It would make pictures by shooting electrons at a special screen.

Philo worked hard on his idea. He tried one **experiment** after another. Some of his teachers helped. They tried new ways of making the tube. The more they tried, the more they learned.

Stop | Think | Write

VOCABULARY

Why do you think Philo had to conduct more than one experiment?

_____

_____

_____

Success!

Finally, the tube was ready. Philo tried to send an image. Can you guess what image he sent? It was a dollar sign.

The tube worked! Philo sent a television image. It was like the ones we see today. He was just twenty-one years old. His **research** and testing were successful. He had made a new kind of television.

Stop Think Write

INFER AND PREDICT

How did Philo's <u>research</u> and testing lead to success?

TV Catches On

Television was getting popular. A large company said that it had invented the new electron tube. A court said that Philo was the inventor.

Philo did not always like television. He thought many shows were bad. Still, television showed important events, too. In 1969, Philo saw the first man walk on the Moon. Before, he would have read this news.

Stop **Think** **Write**

CAUSE AND EFFECT

How did television change the way people learned news?

_____

_____

_____

A Great Inventor

Philo made other inventions. He helped create radar. He thought of a machine that hospitals used to help babies. He found new ways for people to get electricity. He created over 300 inventions!

Philo Farnsworth died in 1971. Today, almost every home has a television. A magazine said Philo was one of the most important people of the twentieth century. Would you agree?

Stop | **Think** | **Write**

CAUSE AND EFFECT

Why did a magazine say that Philo was one of the most important people of the twentieth century?

_____

_____

_____

Look Back and Respond

1 How did Philo become interested in science?

_____

_____

_____

Hint

For clue, see pages 265 and 266.

2 Why was Philo critical of television?

_____

_____

_____

Hint

For clues, see page 269.

3 Do you think Philo cared about helping people? Explain.

_____

_____

_____

Hint

For clues, see page 270.

✓ **TARGET VOCABULARY**

landscape
peak
slopes
steep
textures

Mountains

1 The **landscape** is beautiful. You can see mountains. You can see forests. You can see a river.

Describe the kind of <u>landscape</u> you like best.

_____

_____

_____

2 The mountains are **steep**. It is hard to climb to the top.

Name something other than a mountain that can be <u>steep</u>.

_____

_____

_____

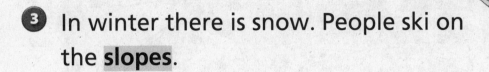

3 In winter there is snow. People ski on the **slopes**.

Which <u>slopes</u> are best for fast skiing—steep ones or gentle ones?

_____

4 Look at that tall **peak**! Snow covers the top of the mountain.

Write a synonym for <u>peak</u>.

_____

5 Snow and ice have different **textures**. Some snow is light and fluffy. Ice is hard and smooth.

Compare the <u>textures</u> of sandpaper and silk.

_____

_____

_____

Climbing the Slopes

by Mia Lewis

It is a sunny day in the Green Mountains. A group of students arrive at a lodge. The **landscape** is beautiful.

"Hi!" says a young man. "I'm Javier. This is Karen. We are going to teach you about rock climbing. We'll also teach you how to find your way in the forest. You'll have a lot of fun this week!"

Stop **Think** **Write**

FACT AND OPINION

Javier says, "You'll have a lot of fun this week!" Is that a fact or an opinion? Explain.

_____

_____

_____

The group meets inside a building. It has a climbing wall. The wall looks like a rock. The wall has different **textures**.

"There's a lot to learn," says Karen. "We're going to practice first."

"That wall is **steep**," says Teo.

"You'll do fine," says Javier. "You just have to practice."

Stop **Think** **Write**

VOCABULARY

What different textures can a rock have?

_____

_____

_____

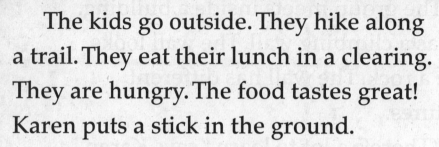

The kids go outside. They hike along a trail. They eat their lunch in a clearing. They are hungry. The food tastes great! Karen puts a stick in the ground.

"What are you doing?" asks Maya.

"I'm going to find out where north, east, south, and west are," she says.

"My cell phone is better. It can show where we are. It has maps," says Teo.

Stop **Think** **Write**

What part of what Teo says is fact? What part is his opinion?

_____

_____

_____

"Your phone can't tell us where north is," says Karen.

"A cell phone could lose power, too," says Latoya. "Then it can't help at all."

"We can use the sun to tell directions," says Karen. "See the shadow of the stick? Let's mark the tip of the shadow with a pebble. Now we wait a while."

Stop | Think | Write

STORY STRUCTURE

Why can't the children use Teo's cell phone to find the direction?

_____

_____

_____

They check after ten minutes. The shadow has moved. Karen puts a pebble where the tip of the shadow is now. She draws a line between the two pebbles.

"The shadow moved because the sun moved," she says. "The sun moves west. Shadows move east. We know which way the shadow moved. So we know which way is east. Now we can follow any directions we have!"

Stop | **Think** | **Write**

CAUSE AND EFFECT

Why does the stick's shadow move?

_____

_____

_____

The next day the students meet again. They stand at the bottom of some rocky **slopes**. Javier is with them. Teo looks worried.

"Are these ropes safe?" he says.

"They are very safe," says Javier. "You did well on the climbing wall. Give it a try. I'll be here to help."

Stop **Think** **Write**

VOCABULARY

What kinds of things can people do on mountain slopes?

_____

_____

_____

A few days later, it is time to go home! Time has passed too quickly.

"I learned so much!" says Maya. "I am going to miss this camp."

"We will miss you, too," says Karen.

"I wish I had time for one last climb," says Teo. "I feel as if I could reach the **peak** of the mountain!"

"You'll just have to come back soon," says Javier.

Stop | Think | Write

Read this sentence: "Time has passed too quickly." Is that a fact or an opinion? Explain your answer.

_____

_____

_____

Look Back and Respond

1 Teo says the climbing wall is too steep. Is that a fact or his opinion?

_____

_____

2 Name a person in the story who mostly expresses opinions. Write one opinion that he or she says.

_____

_____

_____

3 Name a person in the story who mostly states facts. Write one fact that he or she says.

_____

_____

_____

✓ TARGET VOCABULARY

athlete
championship
competitor
rooting
succeed

Working Hard and Having Fun

An **athlete** is someone who plays a sport. Soccer players are athletes. So are tennis players. Athletes train hard to **succeed**. They go to practice. They go to games. They push themselves.

Every **competitor** wants to win, but no one can win all the time! Everyone has good days and bad days.

The last game of the season is the **championship**. The two best teams play. The crowds are **rooting** for their teams. One group cheers for this team. Another group cheers for that team.

1 The _____ is the

last game of the season.

2 A person who plays a sport is an

_____.

3 Athletes train hard to

_____.

4 How does <u>rooting</u> for a team help
the players on that team?

_____

_____

_____

5 When might a <u>competitor</u> not want to
win?

_____

_____

_____

Sprinting Joyce

by Mia Lewis

Joyce had a big brother. His name was Roy. He drove her to school each day. When they arrived, he always said the same thing.

"See you later, slowpoke!"

This was starting to bug Joyce. She had joined the track team. Her coach didn't think she was a slowpoke!

Stop | **Think** | **Write**

UNDERSTANDING CHARACTERS

How does Roy act toward Joyce?

Joyce told her friend Leslie what was going on.

"Roy is the sports editor of the school paper, "said Leslie."I'll write some articles about the team. I'll give you a nickname. I'll say you are a great **athlete**. Roy won't know it's you. Once he finds out, he'll know you aren't a slowpoke."

Joyce smiled."This sounds like fun!"

Stop **Think** **Write**

CAUSE AND EFFECT

How could Leslie's plan change Roy's mind?

_____

_____

_____

Leslie told her plan to the track team.

"From now on," she said, "Joyce will be SJ. It stands for Sprinting Joyce. Don't tell Roy!"

"Your secret is safe!" said Meg and Rita.

"You just have to run fast, Joyce!" said Leslie. "Then our plan will **succeed**."

"I'll try!" said Joyce.

Stop **Think** **Write**

INFER AND PREDICT

Why does Leslie tell the other teammates about the plan?

_____

_____

_____

SPORTS

SJ Makes Team

by Leslie Chin

You can hear the buzz around school. What's it about? It's about our girls' track team. They are fast! They may go to the **championship**. The rising star is SJ.

SJ is leading the team. She is quite a **competitor**!

Stop **Think** **Write**

VOCABULARY

What is the difference between a <u>competitor</u> in a game and the winner?

_____

_____

_____

"Now I have to win!" said Joyce.

"Don't worry," said Leslie. "Just don't tell Roy how fast you run. He'll be so surprised!"

Just then, Roy walked by their table.

"Who is this SJ?" he asked.

"You must be kidding!" Meg said. "Everybody knows SJ!"

Stop **Think** **Write**

CONCLUSIONS AND GENERALIZATIONS

How can you tell that Joyce is a fast runner?

_____

_____

_____

SPORTS

Track Coach Predicts Victory

by Leslie Chin

Get set for a big win! Our girls' track team looks good. SJ is heating up the track. We're all **rooting** for her!

The coach is happy, too. "I think SJ will take us to the top," she said.

"I wish I could tell Roy," said Joyce. "He thinks I'm warming the bench."

"Just run," said Leslie.

Stop **Think** **Write**

VOCABULARY

What does Leslie mean when she writes that everyone is <u>rooting</u> for SJ?

_____

_____

_____

It was time for their next race. Joyce led the team to a big win.

"Did you know that SJ is short for Sprinting Joyce?" Leslie asked Roy.

Roy smiled. "I won't call you slowpoke anymore," he said. "I promise!"

Joyce was happy. Leslie wrote about the race. She chose a headline for the story: "Winning Team Gets Cheers from Roy!"

Stop | Think | Write

UNDERSTANDING CHARACTERS

How does Joyce feel now?

_____

_____

_____

Look Back and Respond

1 How does Roy bother Joyce?

Hint
For a clue, see page 284.

_____

_____

_____

2 Write two words to describe Leslie.

Hint
Think about Leslie's plan and her stories.

_____

_____

_____

3 Write three words to describe Roy.

Hint
Think about how Roy acts at the beginning and at the end.

_____

_____

_____

4 Write a title of your own for Leslie's final story.

Hint
Think about what happens in the story.

_____

_____

_____

Raising Money for a Friend

✓ TARGET VOCABULARY

afford
applause
certainly
raise
worried

It was my friend Rosa's birthday. Rosa loves to draw. Eddie and I wanted to give her crayons. We could not **afford** to buy them. We were **worried**. What could we do?

We decided to **raise** money. We sold lemonade. It was so tasty! We **certainly** had lots of customers. We earned money, too.

Eddie and I got the crayons. Rosa clapped when she saw them. We didn't buy crayons to get **applause**. We just wanted to make Rosa happy.

1 Eddie and I could not _____ to buy crayons.

2 We were _____ about not having money.

3 We did not buy a gift to get

_____ .

4 What is one thing you will <u>certainly</u> do next summer?

_____

_____

_____

5 What are some things you can do to <u>raise</u> money?

_____

_____

_____

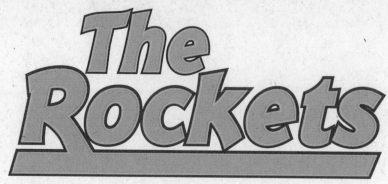

The Rockets

by Candyce Norvell

It was the beginning of the season. Coach Gema was giving the Rockets a speech.

"There are three things we need for a winning team," he said. "We need practice. We need discipline. We need teamwork. I want you all to work with the team. Don't try to be a star on your own. Remember, there's no *I* in *team.*"

Stop Think Write

CONCLUSIONS AND GENERALIZATIONS

Why does Coach Gema want the Rockets to remember that there is no *I* in *team*?

_____

_____

_____

The team worked hard at practice. Soon they were working well as a team. They even won their first game!

Coach Gema was proud. Then he heard some team members brag. "I don't like bragging. Remember what I told you," he said. "There is no I in *team*."

Stop | **Think** | **Write**

CONCLUSIONS AND GENERALIZATIONS

Why doesn't Coach Gema want the team members to show off?

_____

_____

_____

295

One day, Emily told her friend Lupe bad news. Emily had to quit the team. "My mom is sick," Emily said. "My family needs me at home. We all need to help out. We can't afford to pay someone else."

"The team will be sorry to lose you," said Lupe. "You are a great player."

Lupe told the team about Emily.

"I am **worried** about Emily and her family," said Will. "Can the team help?"

Stop | **Think** | **Write**

VOCABULARY

Why is Will worried?

_____

_____

_____

"I know a group that helps families," Anders said. "Maybe we can **raise** money for that group."

"That's a great idea," said Coach Gema. "What should we do?"

"How about a car wash?" said Sovann. "We could have it this weekend."

The whole team agreed.

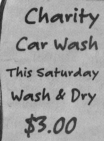

Charity Car Wash
This Saturday
Wash & Dry
$3.00

Stop | **Think** | **Write**

CONCLUSIONS AND GENERALIZATIONS

How do the Rockets feel about Sovann's idea to have a car wash?

_____

_____

_____

On Saturday, the team brought supplies. They washed cars all day. They raised a lot of money. They gave the money to the group that would help Emily's family.

Coach Gema was proud of the Rockets. "You remembered that there is no *I* in *team*," he said.

"Maybe we can earn more money. Let's have a car wash next weekend, too," said Anders.

Stop   Think   Write

INFER AND PREDICT

What do you think the Rockets will do next?

_____

_____

_____

When the season ended, the Rockets went to the school sports dinner.

"There are two more awards to give out," said the principal. "One award is for a team that raised money to help someone. The other award is for the best teamwork. Both awards go to the Rockets! They remembered that there's no *I* in *team*."

Everyone clapped. The Rockets listened to the **applause**. They were proud.

Stop | **Think** | **Write**

VOCABULARY

What is another word for applause?

_____

_____

_____

Later that week, the Rockets went out for pizza.

"I want olives!" said Anders.

"I want extra cheese!" said Lupe.

"I want hot peppers!" Sovann said.

"Not peppers! I want sausage," said Will.

"Hey!" said Coach Gema. "What about teamwork?"

"Coach," Will said. "There is no *I* in *team*, but there is **certainly** an *I* in *pizza*!"

Stop **Think** **Write**

CONCLUSIONS AND GENERALIZATIONS

How do the Rockets act at the pizza place?

_____

_____

_____

Look Back and Respond

1 How do you know that Lupe is a good friend to Emily?

Hint

For clues, see page 296.

_____

_____

_____

2 What shows you that the Rockets know how to work as a team?

Hint

For clues, see pages 295 and 298.

_____

_____

_____

3 Would you like to play for the Rockets? Why or why not?

Hint

Think about how the team members treat each other.

_____

_____

_____

Summarize Strategy

You can **summarize** what you read.

- Tell important ideas in your own words.

- Tell ideas in an order that makes sense.

- Keep the meaning of the text.

- Use only a few sentences.

Analyze/Evaluate Strategy

You can **analyze** and **evaluate** a text. Think carefully about what you read. Form an opinion about it.

1. Think about the text and the author.
   - What are the important facts and ideas?
   - What does the author want you to know?

2. Decide what is important. Then form an opinion.
   - How do you feel about what you read?
   - Do you agree with the author's ideas?

Infer/Predict Strategy

Use clues to figure out what the author does not tell you. Then you are making an **inference**.

Use clues to figure out what will happen next. Then you are making a **prediction**.

Monitor/Clarify Strategy

Monitor what you read. Make sure it makes sense.

Find a way to understand what does not make sense.

- Reread.

- Read ahead.

- Ask questions.

Question Strategy

Ask yourself **questions** as you read.

Look for answers.

Some questions to ask:
- What does the author mean?
- Who or what is this about?
- Why did this happen?
- What is the main idea?

Visualize Strategy

You can **visualize**.
- Make pictures in your mind as you read.
- Use words in the text to help you.
- Make pictures of people, places, things, and actions.

PHOTO CREDITS